Raising an Athlete

Raising an Athlete:

How to Instill Confidence, Build Skills and Inspire a Love of Sport

Jack Perconte

Second Base Publishing

Published by Second Base Publishing, P.O. Box 3012, Lisle, Illinois 60532

Copyright © 2009 by Jack Perconte
All Rights Reserved

Illustrator: Bobby Delaney is a graduate of the American Academy of Art

Perconte, Jack.
    Raising an athlete : how to instill confidence, build
skills and inspire a love of sport / Jack Perconte.
    p. cm.
    LCCN 2008911783
    ISBN-13: 978-0-9793562-2-3
    ISBN-10: 0-9793562-2-9

    1. Sports for children. 2. Parent and child.
3. Sports for children—Social aspects. I. Title.

GV709.2.P46 2009   796'.083
                              QBI08-200020

Dedicated to Mom & Dad

Contents

Introduction: Building Bridges over Troubled Playing Fields

PLAYING SPORTS FOR MANY YEARS, followed by teaching baseball, has consumed much of my life. While playing, from a young age through major league baseball, I have encountered many different styles of coaching along the way. At my sports academy and while watching my children play, I have observed and dealt with many parents and coaches. I am in no way an expert on the subjects of coaching and parenting of young athletes, yet my experiences in coaching and conducting camps, clinics and lessons have given me insights that influenced me to write this book. I have experimented with different teaching techniques, as a parent and coach, in order to arrive at the methods that worked to bring out the best in athletes.

Sports has provided so much enjoyment throughout my life. Sports has also created heartache and many trying times in my life. I was one of the fortunate athletes who lived his dream of playing in the major leagues. My wife and I became parents of three young

Reality Check

sports enthusiasts and I have taught baseball (and life, I hope) to aspiring athletes for twenty-one years.

In this book, I share stories and experiences I had playing professional baseball, teaching sports, and parenting three great kids. I believe the insights I share will benefit parents and coaches. This information will allow your team and kids to remember you in a fun, loving and helpful way, allowing you to live up to the role model you are. Though my background is in baseball, the insights apply to all sports and competitive fields.

Sports competition plays a huge role in our culture. I believe it is the best medium to teach life lessons to our youth. It presents many teaching moments for parents, coaches and players. There are many questions and issues to deal with such as: What should parents do when their child cries? How can parents be more encouraging without pushing their kids too hard? How can sports be more fun? When should a player's parents talk to the coach about decisions involving their child? What should coaches and parents say to their kids after a tough game? How do we prevent burnout in athletes? Should a child play travel ball? What makes a good coach? What can athletes do to make the high school and college team? How do parents and coaches inspire young athletes?

Other issues addressed in this book relate to other concerns parents have, such as these:

"He never wants to work at it."
"I just want her to have fun."
"He won't listen to me."
"My daughter does great in practice, but she can't seem to do it in the games."
"He doesn't have any power."

"He gets so nervous in the game."

"She doesn't want to play anymore."

"He gets so down on himself."

"She can't do it because it's 'in her head'."

"Should we play travel ball?"

"She has no confidence."

"His coach doesn't know anything."

"His high school coach is so negative."

"How do we find a college for my son to play?"

"Can you make him a major leaguer?"

I know parents had the best intentions for their sons and daughters. Like all parents, they were looking for ways to help their kids reach their full potential. Often, without realizing it, they were using words and actions that hindered their children's development. Parents who deal with these issues and concerns efficiently will enjoy their child's career, as they guide them to be "all that they can be."

In addition, I observed and heard many stories, good and bad, pertaining to parents' and kids' experiences with sports. Here is one told to me by one of my students:

Our team was sloshing its way through the season, generally playing uninspired baseball. A new head coach took over the team and was very negative, screaming at every little mistake in a demeaning manner. That negative attitude filtered its way down through the team, parents, other coaches and the entire program. Not a lot of fun was taking place. The head coach's dad came to a game excited and proud to watch his son as a head coach of the well respected school. After the post-game talk with more of the aforementioned negativity, the coach's dad came around the corner.

He walked right up to his son and within earshot of players proceeded to say to his son: "You are exactly the coach that you hated to play for when you were growing up. Remember when you were a kid and you would come home after games and be so upset about how the coach treated you and the team. Now, you are that coach."

This story has a better ending than most of the sports horror stories you normally hear. It is a story that spoke to me in many ways: First, coaches and people in leadership positions do not always realize how they are coming across to others. Second, parents should never stop offering constructive advice to their kids. Third, a coach's attitude will affect many, not just the players. Fourth, negativity rarely, if ever, "inspires" people, especially young athletes.

Then there were these stories:

> The coach of an eleven-year-old team who wanted to win a tournament so badly that he neglected to tell one of his weaker players what time the championship game was, so he didn't have to play him.

> The dad who pulled his son off the team because his son did not get to play the position he wanted him to play.

> The mom who pulled her son away from the field by the shirt collar because he did not seem to be hustling the way she wanted him to.

> The dad who waited until his daughter got in the car after a game before he started yelling at her for her poor performance.

The coach who spit at the umpire.

The fight that broke out on the field.

I could go on forever. Like me, you have probably heard and seen some of the same stories.

Where are the parent and coaching police when we need them? It would be great if we could hire people like the coach's father mentioned earlier to go around the country evaluating coaches and letting them know when they are not serving our kids properly. I do not want to say there is only one way to coach, but there is a big difference between providing constructive advice in a positive way and giving advice in a demeaning manner. If there is a place for that latter style, it definitely belongs at the highest levels of sports and not when young players are just developing and striving to have fun and success. Times have changed since I grew up, and people have become more aware and sensitive to the methods of coaching and parenting. It was common when I grew up for coaches to swear and verbally berate a player without players, fans, or parents raising an eyebrow. Likewise, coaches could get away with getting players' attention on the playing field with some physical contact. Those days are over, and a new set of coaching guidelines are required.

I don't want to paint only a gloomy picture of youth sports. Most coaches and parents are good, supportive and have their kids' best interest in mind. Likewise, there are many great stories of positive coaches and parents who inspire and teach the proper and important values of life, through sports. You will read about some of those positive, fun and uplifting stories in this book. It is unfortunate, though, that a small percentage of parents and coaches give sports a bad reputation. Also unfortunate, the negative stories travel much faster than the good stories. A common thought in circulation says that "parents ruin it for the kids." This is true in some instances, but it does not need to be that way. This book is for coaches and parents who want to learn how to make a positive difference in their team and child's life. Whenever I talk of coaches in this book, I am talking to coaches of teams as well as coaches of individuals. Coaches are teachers for teams, and parents are teachers of individuals (their kids). They are both in positions of authority and influence, and both have a life-long effect on young athletes. A saying from an unknown source that I would often repeat at coaching clinics sums up this thought, "A year or two from now, your players will not remember what you taught them; but they will forever remember how you made them feel."

There Will Be Tears

A Very Long Day

My son had hoped to be chosen in the major league draft, but it did not happen. It was a tough day for him, and just as tough for mom and dad. When your own child's dreams appear to be over, the tears will flow. Having played the game at the highest level, I always played with some nervousness. The nervousness of playing at the highest level was different and nothing like the anxieties of watching and hoping for the best for my own kid's dreams, especially when you know it is the activity they love. Parents have some anxiety watching their kids perform at a young age, and the anxiety level grows a little each year their kids stay involved in sports. As the competition level increases each year, there is added anxiety, wondering if your child will keep up and whether this may be the last year that he or she will be good enough or want to continue playing.

Playing with Pressure

I like to think we had prepared our son so he could move on without playing professional baseball, if indeed, that was the end of his career. After all, that is what parents do. They prepare their kids for the highs and lows of sport and for that inevitable day when their careers end. Often, this preparation is difficult for parents who, like most, share in their kid's dreams and career, but they must do it.

Fortunately, we avoided that end, for now at least. A couple days after the baseball draft, our son signed a professional contract. Once again, there were tears, but this time they were tears of joy.

Trials and Tribulations

All athletes encounter difficult times. Inevitably, there will be times when their results do not meet their own and others' expectations. Sports can be very humbling, both for players and parents. At times, everyone feels bad and helpless, not knowing what to do. Keeping things in perspective is essential when dealing with a lack of success. You need to understand bad times come and go and when players struggle on the playing field, it is no time to panic. Keeping an upbeat attitude in front of your kids is important. When kids who are struggling on the field realize their parents are not "panicking," it helps them overcome the tough times. Great athletes look at adversity as a challenge to work harder and to conquer the present obstacle. Portraying that attitude to their kids is good practice for parents.

I can recall many examples of young players who were very successful and flowered with much adoration. However, they quit their sport at a relatively young age, because they could not cope during rough times. Too much attention can cause young players to get too full of themselves, and this can be harmful. Players who are constantly told how great they are often become self-centered and have a hard time adjusting to difficult sports and life situations. Having a star player can become difficult for parents too. These parents get used to having a winning player and have a difficult time dealing with the situation when their kid is no longer a star or no longer playing at all. Being happy with a child's success is fine, but going overboard with attention to one's own kid is unproductive. Constantly praising children over their performance and rewarding them with gifts because of their play are signs of going overboard. Likewise, moms and dads bragging about their children to others too much is a turnoff. No one likes to hear an abundance of talk about how great another parent's son or daughter is doing, except for the child's grandparents.

This is not to say that parents should not praise their kids. It is good to praise them and let them know you are proud of them. It is good to let them know you want them to succeed and you will help them find ways of improving. Just don't go overboard.

Not Just a Game

Anybody who has been involved in sports realizes that it is not all fun and games. There is hard work, failure and disappointment. How can we ever forget the famous line from the movie, *A League of Their Own*, when Tom Hanks whines, "There's no crying in baseball?" Obviously, that statement is not true. Athletes compete, and the dictionary definition of competition—"contention of two or more for the same object or superiority"—suggests a struggle with a winner and loser, in and of itself. Athletes are very passionate and determined and when things do not go their way, the emotions come pouring out. Most people see that in the grand scheme of things, sports and games are not life or death, but they do captivate our interest and bring out our support and emotions. When we see a famous athlete retire and get very emotional, we shake our head and say, "It's just a game." Well, yes, but when people pour their heart, hard work, and life into something they love, there will be tears; and to get to the top, love, focus and passion were needed. These three—love, focus, and passion—produce various emotions ranging from jubilation to despair. People share with athletes the good times, and that is usually enjoyable for all. However, when the emotion produced is sadness, it is not enjoyable and support is necessary to help athletes and parents.

Concerned parents would often say to me, "My son or daughter gets so down on himself/herself." There can be many reasons for this, many of which I will discuss below. The most important thing for parents to do is to make sure that it is not the parent's words or actions that are causing the child to "get so down." Much in this book details ways parents can help kids overcome these upsetting situations. The following are ways of supporting and alleviating the extreme disappointment which brings on the tears.

Coming Through in the Clutch

"I have a new favorite major league player," Joe said to his wife after attending a big league game with his son.

"Why is that?" she asked.

"Well, Derek Lee struck out three times tonight, and he is now my favorite," Joe remarked.

"That makes no sense, you love the Cubs, and even I know that three strike-outs are not good," she said.

"Yes, but you know how Bradley (their son) has been crying after he strikes out?"

"Sure," she replied.

"Well, after the game Bradley says to me, 'Dad, I guess striking out isn't so bad. Derek Lee does it all the time and he is the greatest'."

Players Cry Because They Do Not Perform Up to Their Own Expectations

Everyone has a different personality and shows emotions differently. Some players handle failure by getting angry, some act as if they do not care, some blame others, and some cry. Of these possibilities, the crying player is not so bad and usually it's something that a little "tender loving care" can take care of.

 Things Parents Can Do:

❖ After a tough game, say "Hang in there, we'll figure it out." *We* is a powerful word that will let your child know you are there to help and they do not have to figure out the lack of success on their own.

❖ Always point out little signs of improvement, even if it is not showing up in game results.

❖ Stay positive and try something helpful. Having the player perform some basic fundamental drills at home or at the field can show immediate results. Look up some drills in books, videos, or online to give the player some constructive things to work on. The player's coach can provide a few drills to help the player too.

✧ It is difficult for parents to have much empathy for their upset child when the young player did not practice and prepare much. Some players have yet to connect the idea that results only come with hard work. Be delicate about how you say things, but explain to the player that better results will come when he or she puts greater preparation into it. For players who did prepare, tell them good results will come soon and you are proud of their hard work.

✧ Have your child get help from a knowledgeable or professional instructor. Knowledge creates confidence, which creates success and a happier player. For younger players, parents should attend the instructional sessions to learn what to work on with their sons or daughters.

It's Not Always What You Think

"Good news today, Mary," said Mary's husband on the phone.

"Why is that?" she asked.

"Michelle came home from practice and was happy for once and never said anything negative about her coach. I asked her what was up, and she said Tina (another player trying out for the team) was cut today."

"Why would that make her happy?" Mary asked.

"It seems the coach never said anything to Tina, and the coach was always yelling at Michelle. Michelle thought the coach didn't like her and would cut her. She now realizes the coach was yelling at her because she has a chance to be good, and the coach ignored Tina because she didn't see any potential in her."

Players Cry Because the Coach "Isn't A Good Coach" (at least in the player's mind)

When tension develops between the coach and the player, the parent is in a tough spot. Listen to your child and try to understand their feelings.

 Things Parents Can Do:

- ✧ First, parents must be careful not to create a bad situation. Often, parents start grumbling about the coach in front of the young player. Parents should watch their own comments and attitudes. More often than not, the players are happy playing, having fun, and being around their teammates, and only become disenchanted with their coach when Mom and Dad are not satisfied

- ✧ Most concerns revolve around playing time, positions played, or perceived personality conflicts. If your child's concerns need addressing with the coach, approach the coach in a private setting, away from all players and fans. Discuss the situation like adults. Alienating the coaching staff can make for a very long season. Do not expect the volunteer coach to be an expert and remember your child is part of a team. I hope the coach has the best interests of all the players at heart and an understanding is reached. Do not tell your kid that you talked with the coach, because this will make the child feel worse and self-conscious around the coach.

- ✧ Encourage your son or daughter to work extra hard at practice. Most coaches will appreciate the extra work effort and reward the player. Also, encourage your child to do little things like picking up equipment at the end of practice. This makes a good impression on the coach and may help the situation.

✧ Explain to your child that in the end, she will be a better person for the experience and she should not blame "the sport" for the problem with the coach.

✧ If your child is interested, having him attend an outside clinic or camp can bring back the fun of the game. Generally, camps are instructional in nature with an emphasis on improvement and fun.

Talent Driven Away

I could not wait to ask him. I had not seen my old friend for eight years, after he moved away at the age of twelve. You see, my friend Gary would practically beg me to ask his dad if he could come over to my house, after every game. He said his dad would let him if I asked him. So, I would. Gary going home with me immediately after games became a regular occurrence. I never knew why it was so important to him.

We finally were meeting, after all that time, at a college football game. After awhile, I worked up the nerve to ask him why he always insisted on coming home with me after the games. After a slight hesitation, he said, "the fifteen-minute drive home with my dad after games was the worst time of my life. My dad was never satisfied with how I played, and he would let me know it. I couldn't stand it and never played sports again after we moved away."

Players Cry Because Their Parents Put Too Much Pressure On Them to Succeed

L. Ron Hubbard said, "The biggest mistake an athlete can make is to be afraid to make one." Parental pressure on young players is a given. Some parents place more pressure on their kids than others do, but it is always there and it may put a big strain on relationships.

 Things Parents Can Do:

✧ After a game, ask "Did you have fun?" Let the player talk about the game if they want to, but don't start telling them things they did wrong. Parents will create tension if they immediately start asking why they did or did not do something in the game. Talk about other events of the day too. Revisit their performance later, either after dinner or the next day. Provide some positive ideas for improvement at this later time.

✧ The same goes when practicing together—do not immediately start giving instructions. Allow for a warm-up time and for a few mistakes before giving some constructive suggestions.

✧ Speak in a matter-of-fact voice when giving instructions, and save the emotional voice for when they do it correctly. It is always better to describe the action. For example, saying "that last throw or swing wasn't correct" is better than saying "you cannot do it that way." Placing too much emphasis on every game can put unwanted stress on young athletes. "Being there" for them does not mean parents have to physically be at every game.

✧ If the child seems to be more nervous when the parent is at the game, and is not having as much fun as they do at practice, the parent should miss a game from time to time or watch the game from a distance. This can help the child realize their performance isn't the most important thing in their parent's day, or life. It may be just the game pressure which is causing the extra nervousness, but it is worth finding out what is causing it. Most of all, parents should avoid the looks of disgust, the look away, the rolling of eyes, the words under the breath, and the negative comments when the player is practicing or playing.

Wasted Energy

Story in today's *Herald News*: Central High's championship chances took a hit today when its star player broke his hand and is out for the season. Unfortunately, he did not become injured in the game, but afterward when he punched his locker after the win because he was not happy with his own performance. This can serve as a good lesson for all young players; this young player has not only hurt himself but has also let his team, school, and city down.

Players Cry Because They Put Too Much Pressure on Themselves

The player who thrives on doing well and has trouble dealing with failure may be the toughest one to deal with. This is a delicate situation because these types of players are usually very hard workers and passionate about the game. The parent certainly does not want to take that work ethic and passion away.

Things Parents Can Do:

- Examine the situation fully to make sure that you, the parents, are not putting undue pressure on the player. Talk to your child and ask questions. Explain that no athlete can star in every game and you certainly do not expect this of them.

- Do not allow embarrassing behavior on the field. Parents should not allow fits of temper or getting mad at umpires, coaches, or other players. The parent may have to threaten to have the player miss the next game if the behavior continues. Follow through with the threat if the situation does not change, but do not give up on the player. Many great players started out with anger problems, only to go on to greatness after they learned to control their anger.

- Give the player a little time to sulk after the game, but do not allow throwing things, swearing or negative comments about themselves or others. Most players will come around after a short time and a good meal. Try to get the player's mind off his or her performance as soon as possible, and only return to it later if the player brings it up.

- Tell the player you believe in them and they should believe in themselves. Stay positive with the player and have patience. However, do not overdo the praise. They will recognize false praise and tune it out or get upset.

- Talk to the player's coach about the situation. Ask the coach to have patience with the player and look for ways to ease the self-pressure. Getting this player to smile out on the playing field from time to time can be a great help, allowing the player to relax.

Winning with Dignity

It was a devastating loss for the 13-year-old team. The winning team would be going to California for the world championship. They did not win and players were upset and crying after the game. Nothing the coaches said seemed to help the situation. After a while, the coaches and players from the winning team came over. The coach from the winning team said, "We are having a picnic and then going to the water park and we would like your team to join us." The coaches on the losing team were now overwhelmed and this gesture brought a tear to their eyes too. They accepted and all had a great time. When the winning team returned from California, the coaches of the losing team invited the winning team over for a celebration of both team's season.

Players Cry Because They Lose the Game

There has to be a winner and a loser. Coaches and parents should be role models for their players and should handle winning and losing with grace and dignity. The players will recognize the adults' behavior and follow their example.

 Things Parents and Coaches Can Do:

- ✦ Watch for exhausted players. Players who play too many games in a day or week become physically and emotionally exhausted. This is more common these days because of the greater emphasis on travel teams. Give the players a few days away from the game to rest and clear their minds.

- ✦ Focus on the effort level of the players after games, not on the result. The postgame talk should include a short review of what the team will work on at the next practice (based on what they saw in the game), a high-five and a smile.

✦ Instruct in practice and before games, but leave the games just for playing. Most pressure occurs in the game. It is not the time for coaches to be yelling out too much instruction.

✦ Do not use rewards for winning or penalize the team for losing. Examples of this are promising a trip to the players' favorite restaurant as an incentive if they win or threatening to make the team run if the team loses.

✦ Teach the players about the things they can control—their mental and physical preparation—and they cannot always control the outcome.

Booster "Shot"

Almost everyone knows Michael Jordan did not make the basketball team one year of high school, only to eventually become the greatest player of all time. That story is an inspiration for many, but not the outcome that happens for most. Once cut from a team, a player often is finished in that sport.

Matt worried he would not make his high school team. He worried because of the warning sign from the season before. He did not play very well and lost the starting job to another player. At best, he thought he would be on the bench, even if he made the team. Opposed to sitting the bench, Matt decided against trying out for the team. He was content with his decision, especially because of what happened the previous season. It was the last game of the season when Matt pinch hit, and the unthinkable happened, a true moment right out of the movie "The Natural." Matt, who had never hit a homerun in his life, hit the ball out of the park. The homerun actually hit the scoreboard. He insists to this day there is a dent in the scoreboard. Friends and family ask him, facetiously, if lightning and thunder came because of the homerun too. The best part of the story is the pride and self-worth that home run produced in Matt's personality. His parents believe "the hit" gave him the feeling that "anything is possible" and it made playing the sport all those years worthwhile in his development to adulthood.

Parents and Players Both Cry Because the Player Does Not Make the Team

This is a tough time for the whole family.

 Things Parents Can Do:

 ✧ Prepare before the tryout for the eventuality that your child may not make the team. If sports teach us anything, it is we should assume nothing. Encourage the player to work hard and take the tryout seriously so they will have few regrets if things do not work out. Tell them to do their best, and that is all anyone can expect of them.

 ✧ It may be necessary to check with the coach as to why your child did not make the team. Do this in a polite way, realizing the coach has a tough job deciding on who to keep and who to cut. Bridge burning is never good—the player may be able to try out for the same team in the future or may get a call if another player drops off the team.

 ✧ Ask the coach what areas your child needs to improve in and for any tips to help them go about that.

✧ Tell your child stories like the one about Michael Jordan. Encourage them to keep playing and practicing, if they so desire, because the outcome can be different the next time.

✧ Explore all the possible playing options that may be available, especially for the player who does not seem to be getting over the disappointment after a day or two. For younger players there are always other teams and leagues to consider. Sometimes, the other options turn out to be a better experience anyway.

✧ It can be an extremely trying time for high school players who do not make the team, because it could mean the end of their playing opportunities. If that is the case, look for other alternatives to keep the player involved if they truly love the sport. Becoming the team equipment manager, statistician, or announcer may be possible alternatives to keep the player around his friends and a part of the team.

Keeping it in Perspective

Brad's mom could not take it anymore. She walked into the house, went up to her room, and started crying. Soon after, her husband walked in and asked what was wrong. She said she was upset because their son had another terrible game that day and she felt so bad for him. She went on to say how terrible their son felt and she did not know what to do to help. Her husband volunteered to go talk to him. He walked into their son's room only to hear his son excitedly say, "Dad, watch this, I'm beating the video game of Mario!"

**Parents Cry Because They Do Not Know How
to Help Their Struggling Young Ball Player.**

The game creates tension for parents too. As the parents in the previous story learned, though, many young players are more resilient than parents realize. Although they may be very disappointed in their child's play, parents should understand they might be taking their kid's results much harder than the young player is. Keeping a good perspective is important for parents. The good news is that over time, sports develops resiliency in athletes and parents.

Things Parents Can Do:

- ✧ Parents can find time to work with their son or daughter as soon after games as possible, as long as the child is interested. Both parent and child will feel better by being proactive and not dwelling on the bad game. This puts the emphasis on the next game, instead of reflecting on the last one and keeps everybody positive and hopeful. For parents who do not have the time or expertise to help, enroll the child in private lessons, clinics, or camps. Parents will have peace of mind knowing they are doing everything possible to help their child succeed.

- ✧ If a parent does need to cry because of their child's upsetting situation, they should do it out of sight of their child. In addition, ignoring their child when they do not perform up to their expectations is never a good practice.

- ✧ Communicate concerns with each other (husband and wife) when there is tension between a child and one of the parents. A parent may not recognize the tension they are creating and pointing this out can be helpful.

✧ Never force kids to practice, but continue to explain that good results come with hard work. Instilling the importance of a good work ethic in their sons and daughters is one of the most important lessons the parent can give their kids. A good work ethic will serve them in every area of their future. Learning ways of making practice fun can be a great help also.

✧ Most of all, parents should not relive their playing days through their kids. Recognizing their kids are unique individuals who must be themselves allows the kids the freedom to grow as athletes and people. It is important for kids to realize they are so much more than how they perform on a playing field.

Reality Check

I encourage parents to have realistic goals for their kids and understand the chances of making it to the professional level are miniscule. Encouraging kids to dream and have goals is great, as long as parents also encourage perspective, realism, and other interests. A time may come for the elite athlete to apply complete focus and passion to his or her efforts, but that will be up to the player and beyond the responsibility of the parents. The parents' responsibility is to encourage their children and to promote many interests, especially emphasizing the need for a good education. I have seen many kids that believe their sporting prowess will eventually turn into a pro career and millions of dollars, only to see their career end with nothing to fall back on. Parents and coaches are responsible for explaining and insisting on the importance of not risking everything on one endeavor. Eventually, the ability to play competitive sports ends for all athletes, even the great, professional ones. All these athletes need something to fall back on to continue to grow as a person. Stressing the importance of education is an ongoing responsibility for parents.

The Exception

A parent came into my academy one day and began talking. He mentioned that a baseball coach had told him his high school sophomore son was going to be the next Mickey Mantle, and he seemed to believe that also. Of course, my first thought, which I did not state, was "get real, Mister." When he did bring his boy in, I noticed his son had enormous talent, a great work ethic, and dedication. Of course, he did not have Mickey Mantle talent (no one does), but the young player went on to become a very fine major league player. The point is, parents and coaches should never take away, discourage, or doubt players' goals. It is ok to present the realities of the obstacles and chances to reach the goals, but no one should deny players their dreams and goals.

A Parent's Wisdom

You may recall the story about baseball Hall-of-Famer Mickey Mantle. "The Mick" was struggling when he first began professional baseball and was probably home-sick too. He called home and told his dad he'd had enough, that he couldn't hit and was not enjoying himself. His dad immediately showed up at Mick's door, coming from many miles away. Mickey asked his dad why he was there and his dad said, "I came to pack up your stuff, because the game seems too tough for you, and I have a job for you down in the coal mine with me." Now, Mickey realized what tough was and how good he had it to be able to play. The rest is history.

Parents and young players should realize just because things do not go their way is no reason to quit the team or stop working on the game. There is another less famous quotation from the movie, *A League of Their Own,* that says, "It is supposed to be hard. If it wasn't hard, everyone would do it. The hard . . . is what makes it great." This is true and another point to make to ballplayers. Success is not easy and, parents especially, should keep this in mind as their kids play youth sports. If your son or daughter enjoy playing, encourage them to keep playing, even if they are not very successful. The result may not be the big leagues, but it will provide happy times and being around the game they love.

Career Building

Where Dreams Begin

IT IS NOT A COINCIDENCE that the sons and daughters of professional athletes follow in their parent's footsteps. Those kids were around the sport from the day they were born. Those early years, around the sport, shaped their futures. I don't know when I first decided I wanted to be a major league ballplayer, but one of the only memories I have before the age of six was of going to a major league baseball game with my dad. I can still picture a New York Yankee right fielder (probably Roger Maris) making a tremendous throw to home plate against the Chicago White Sox. That may have been the day my dream started.

I was no different from many young players of yesterday and today with that dream. Many kids at a young age dream of and have the goal of becoming a professional ball player. At a young age, sports are fun, and for many, success comes easily at first.

Keeping It in Perspective

In addition, kids notice the notoriety and awe that great athletes receive, so it is easy to develop this dream.

When kids first begin to play sports, it is common for parents, also, to dream of their kid becoming a professional star. That is ok, but many parents create potential problems down the line when they believe their aspirations are the same as their child's desires. It is important for parents to understand their role is not to impose their dreams and goals on their kids but to foster their child's interests. Kids need time to sort out what their favorite activities are, and as they are doing this, parents should provide the help their kids need to develop their talents. Parents can do this by showing interest in their child's interests, providing encouragement and financial support, if possible.

Definition of Perspective

This word *perspective* and the concept of "keeping it in perspective" are often associated with sports. It is important that people understand these terms. The problem is that perspective is rarely defined, and exactly what "in perspective" means is often unclear. In addition, whose perspectives are we talking about is another vague area. I was guilty of this in the previous chapter when I assumed everyone understood what I meant when I said things should be kept "in perspective." One dictionary definition of perspective is "a distant view," which implies the idea of looking from the outside in at the overall picture. Keeping something "in perspective" implies people can step back and look at a situation from a distance to arrive at the proper course of action. That is exactly why the term appears so often in sports, because all too often people involved with youth sports do not "step back" and look at the overall picture before acting. Their impulsive behavior often leads to hurt feelings and the negative stories that give sports a bad reputation.

It is necessary to keep life passions like sports in perspective. However, what "keeping it in perspective" means for one person can be different from another person's view. With this in mind, the following is a definition of keeping it in perspective as far as sports are concerned.

- ✧ Always keep in mind the age of the players.
- ✧ Ensuring the physical and emotional health of the child is always most important.
- ✧ Realizing that sports are only games and one aspect of many aspects of a child's life, and not the most important one.
- ✧ Always remembering that it is the player's, not the adults, career.
- ✧ Understanding competition creates emotions, but these emotions should never override good judgment about the four previous points.

As mentioned, not everyone is coming from the same perspective. So, it is necessary for people to communicate with each other about their perspectives, in an adult manner, so players and teams have positive playing experiences throughout their careers.

The Young and Innocent

The following is a journal entry from a young ballplayer that has a healthy view of perspective:

Dear Diary,

My coach is constantly yelling at me to "concentrate." I am most of the time, but every time I see an airplane, a bug, or a friend, my mind wanders and I forget where I am. The other day when a play was coming my way, I was helping a bug get out of the way. Coach yelled and yelled at me, but I could not have lived with myself if someone would have squashed that bug.

My mom is always saying "just have fun" when I'm playing. I think I am, especially when my friend Jimmy and I are talking and fooling around on the bench when our coach is not paying attention to us. It is really fun after the games when we go out for ice cream too. I really have fun when I play the game on the Wii at home because I actually do well and no one is screaming at me all the time to "do this or that."

Dad gets so upset with me during and after the games. He cannot believe I am not better, and he keeps telling me how easy it was for him and that he used to be an all-star every year. I did challenge him to play with me at the video, and he got mad when I beat him. I know I should not have said, "I cannot believe you are that bad at this." It would have been ok, but then I said, "When I was younger, I used to practice and play this video game all the time." Oh well.

I plan to start concentrating, practicing and having more fun playing the regular game as soon as I finish this Harry Potter book I am reading.

That is all for now.

Parents may not be able to determine their child's ultimate life interests, but they certainly can influence their child's early interests. The years between three and seven years old are the time when interest for an activity usually is developed. These early interests may lead to the love of that activity. When kids do not develop a liking for an activity at an early age, especially something as difficult as sports, they usually drop out when the competition level greatly improves between the ages of ten and twelve.

Ages Three through Seven: Developing the Love

Parents should introduce several interests and several sports to kids at these ages. Playing sports at a young age is good, yet too much of one sport at this age can lead to burnout or boredom for the young player. Often, kids will play the sport they are seeing on TV, which is usually the sport of that season of the year. The sports the parent wants their child to be most interested in should get some extra attention. There is no guarantee the child will develop a love for that sport down the line, but there is a better chance when parents show their enthusiasm for the particular sport or sports of choice.

 Things Parents Can Do:

✦ Go to games with kids—high school, college and professional games are all good. Bring along equipment to play a little during games when possible. This is important because young players may get bored watching after awhile so be prepared for some action.

✦ Watch the sport on TV—call kids in to see the exciting plays if they are not watching.

✧ Talk about the sport from time to time, even in the off-season. Do not overdo it, but try to create conversation about it.

✧ Buy video games of that sport for the kids. Play the video game with your children if they want you to.

✧ Play the sport with your child whenever they want to, when either you or they suggest it. Do not force them to play, and try to eliminate the tedious parts for younger ages. (For example, in baseball: when players are learning to catch the ball, use a soft ball that won't hurt if it hits them, and have the players stand in front of a backstop so they are not constantly chasing missed balls.) Common-sense adjustments like these to keep the playing enjoyable are a great help at these young ages.

✧ Teach a few basics, yet do not overwhelm the child with instruction. Keep it simple, but try to demonstrate the correct way to do things with your actions. Kids will subconsciously do what they see.

✧ Play as long as the child wants, within reason. The parent should not be the one to stop playing.

✧ Make play fun. Positive talk, encouraging words, and game-like situations are fun.

✧ Show excitement when they do something good. Kids enjoy doing things that make mom and dad happy.

Ages Eight through Twelve: Developing the Skills and Knowledge of the Game

It is very difficult to break bad habits, and the habits formed at a young age will be especially difficult to change. Between ages eight and twelve, parents should focus on giving their kids good instruction. Players who are good players at these young ages are usually the ones who are good at the older level of youth sports also.

Things Adults Can Do to Develop Young Athletes:

- ✧ Continue the things begun in the above section (ages three through seven).
- ✧ Teach the fundamentals—keep it simple but stay persistent. (Many coaches tell players how to perform the skills, but then allow them to do them incorrectly.)
- ✧ Drill work and repetition are very important to develop consistency and confidence.
- ✧ Challenge players up to a point, but do not let frustration set in. End practice sessions on a high note. (A few good plays, for example).
- ✧ Along with learning the skills of the game, parents and coaches should teach the tactics and strategies of the game to the players. Learning what to do in game situations is as important for a player's development as learning the skills.
- ✧ Along with their regular team practices, having players attend camps, clinics, or lessons from time to time is good. Do not overdo it, but it is important that players learn the correct fundamentals. Learning to take instruction from others, and not just mom or dad, is good too.
- ✧ Playing the sport occasionally in the offseason just to keep the sport somewhat in the player's mind is good. (An example is getting the gloves out to play a little catch in the winter.)

✧ As the player enters organized leagues, it is important that parents put the player at the correct level for the player's skill level. Sometimes, league rules will dictate what level the child must play.

✧ Consider the option of playing travel ball. Generally, it is too early for players to specialize at these ages, but it is good to take extra practice with the player's favorite sport.

✧ Be patient and positive, always recognizing little improvements and praising hard work.

As kids reach the teenage years, some difficult decisions present themselves for players and parents:

Ages Thirteen through Sixteen: Decision Time—Quitting, Making the High School Team, and Specialization

It is very common for players to want to quit playing at these ages, especially at age thirteen. Studies have shown that about 70% of players drop out of competitive sports at that age. This can be tough on parents who want their kids to continue playing. Having a good conversation with them about their interest level at this age can be helpful. For kids who no longer wish to continue playing, find out their reasons for wanting to quit. Be understanding, yet encourage them to keep thinking it over. It is common for kids to think they do not want to play, and then wish they had once the season for that sport arrives. If a player's reason for not playing is they just do not enjoy it anymore, then that should be understandable to the parent, although the reason and decision may be disappointing to them. However, if the player wants to quit because he or she feels too small, does not like the coach, or is not good enough, encourage the young person to keep playing because those situations can change in the future.

Things To Do for Kids Who Continue Playing:

✧ Often, at these ages, kids do not want to receive instruction from mom and dad, or a parent's knowledge of the game is not sufficient for this advanced level. In either case, finding a good personal coach can be helpful.

✧ Players should practice their skills for nine months of the year. Conditioning workouts, even for as little as ten minutes per day, each day, should be done. Players playing other sports can count that activity as part of their training.

✧ Players should attend the local high school's camps and should ask the coach for an evaluation as to what they need to work on to improve.

✧ A weight-training program should be encouraged for players.

✧ As always, and especially at these ages, parents should emphasize the importance of grades and good schoolwork habits. Good grades from the beginning of high school are very important for all, especially for the college-bound athletes. It is difficult to raise the grade point average after a bad start.

✧ Players should definitely consider playing travel ball at this time. (See section on travel ball.)

✧ Having a good team coach at this age can make all the difference as to whether the player will want to continue playing. Having your son or daughter try out for teams that have good coaches is worthwhile.

High-School Tryouts

Unfortunately, for many players, large high schools mean more kids try out, fewer make the team, and playing time may be hard to come by.

 Suggestions for Making the High-School Team:

*   ❖ Skill. There is no substitute for talent. All the practice and playing the player has done up to this point should show up in the tryout. Players who have waited too long to get serious about the sport are at a disadvantage.
*   ❖ Size and strength. Unfortunately, bigger kids have an advantage. Smaller kids can overcome their lack of size with strength training, hustle, good fundamental skills, and an acute knowledge of the game.
*   ❖ Attitude. Coaches like "coachable" players. Players should be encouraged to pay attention to the coach's suggestions with eye contact, head nods, good body language, enthusiasm, and trying the suggested pointers from the coaches. Players should not say things to the coach like "I do it this way" or "my dad told me to do this." High school coaches believe they know more than your dad does and they are usually correct. Players who "screw around" and do not seem committed to the sport are at a great disadvantage for making the team and getting playing time. Remind players of the saying that "perception is reality" and their outward attitude, words, and actions are important.
*   ❖ Grades. Coaches like players who care about their schoolwork. They feel kids who work at their schoolwork will work on their game and will remain academically eligible.

❖ Game aptitude. Coaches like players who are "students of the game." Kids who have good instincts and know the finer points of the game have an advantage.

❖ Be on time. Nothing perturbs a coach more than players who show up late for practice.

Specialization

One of the toughest decisions players face is whether to specialize and play one sport or continue playing more than one. Years ago, it was common for the better athletes to play two or three sports in high school. It is rare to see three-sport athletes nowadays, at least at the larger high schools. Whether to specialize or not is a tough call. On one hand, a player enjoys playing two or three sports. On the other hand is the possibility of greater improvement by specializing, which may lead to a college or pro career. Additionally, the lure and competition for college scholarships is at an all-time high. Players who have college potential must consider if and when they should specialize. Whether to specialize can be an even more difficult decision when the sport the player enjoys playing the most is not the sport in which he or she is most successful, or the sport that offers a chance for a scholarship.

Parents and players should analyze their situation by getting input from other parents, coaches, and respected friends. Getting realistic opinions about the player's potential in their best sport is important in making an educated decision. From my experience with multisport athletes, I believe it is best to continue playing other sports as long as the player still enjoys them. More often than not, players who quit other sports only to work on one, end up putting so much pressure on themselves to justify their decision that all the extra work doesn't pay off anyway. Additionally, there is no guarantee the player will show greater improvement just because of the increased work. When a player is talented, that talent will show up later whether they specialize at a young age or not. Ultimately, the player should make the decision based on his desires, so he does not look back with regrets.

Ages Seventeen and Eighteen: College

For the special athletes who have made it this far, it is quite an accomplishment. To play a sport and get good grades through high school is something a player and his family should be very proud of achieving. Many of these student athletes will know that for them, high school sports are the end of the road for competitive sports. They realize they have made it as far as their talent will take them. Other high school graduating athletes may have the talent to play in college, but have had enough playing and want to focus their energies elsewhere after high school. Players who are interested in playing at the college level should understand it requires a great deal of commitment to play a sport and do the college work necessary to get a good education.

College athletic scholarships are very hard to come by, and players should not assume they have landed one until it is a done deal. Star high school players will generally have colleges coming after them, so they will not have to do as much searching for the right college as the non-star player. These non-star players who wish to play in college will have to do the college search themselves. They should not give up their desire to play just because the colleges do not come after them. Many good players can find an interested college, whether they get a scholarship or not, if they are willing to do the groundwork to find a suitable college athletic program. These players, who love to play and have talent and desire, can find a college where they can at least get a tryout. However, it is important that all players find a school that fits their interests in all areas (academically, socially, etc.), because the college experience should be more than just playing sports.

Things Parents and Athletes Interested in Playing at the Collegiate Level Can Do to Increase their Opportunity:

✧ Do not assume the high school coach will do the work to find the player a college. Some high school coaches help more than others do, but parents and players should prepare to do the work, and they should prepare early in the player's high school career.

✧ Parents of players who want to play ball in college should begin networking around sophomore year. Parents should talk to friends, coworkers, coaches, and college alumni about colleges and college athletic programs. Often, contacts lead to a tip or contact from someone that has a college connection. This may lead to an eventual playing opportunity at the next level. Because college coaches are overwhelmed with letters and calls and do not have time to see everybody, they often rely on recommendations from former players and friends. Parents should not brag about their son or daughter to those contacts, but they can state their kid has advanced skill and interest in playing at the next level. Networking can make all the difference for getting an opportunity to play at the collegiate level.

✧ Before junior year, begin to look at colleges that seem to be a good academic and playing fit. Find three to five schools at each level of college ball. Junior college, Division 1, 2, 3 and NAIA are all levels of collegiate competition that are options. Players and parents should become familiar with the different rules of each level. Discuss the distance from home the player is willing to go and the cost of the various colleges. It is important to consider all levels of play until the level most appropriate for the player gets sorted out over the next couple of years.

✧ During junior and senior year, meet with the player's high school coaches and summer coaches to discuss their opinion on what level the player would be best suited. It can be difficult to know which level a player is capable of competing at in college, so as much input as possible from others is usually beneficial. Ask the coach if he or she is willing to send a letter of recommendation, if necessary.

✧ Players should attend a reputable showcase or two, especially before senior year. Showcases are tryout camps where players get evaluations from and exposure to college or professional teams. Showcase exposure often leads to direct or indirect recommendations to college coaches. Parents and players have a tendency to over-rate their kid's talent, so an outside, unbiased opinion from a showcase can be valuable information also. However, parents should be sure the showcase is reputable and not just a "money grab."

✧ Right before or during junior year, send out letters to the college coaches of the schools of interest and state your player's interest in the school.

✧ Send ACT and SAT scores, when available, to the schools of interest.

❖ Keep college coaches up to date with your playing accomplishments and be prepared to follow up with any requests for video or scheduling information.

❖ Playing travel ball the season before graduating can be valuable because of the added exposure travel ball presents. It takes only one coach to have an interest in a player that can make the difference with getting an opportunity at the next level.

❖ Plan to attend the sports camps at the desired colleges. It provides an opportunity to impress the coaches and shows the player's interest in their school. A coach may give the player a good indication of the school's interest in the player also.

❖ Players and parents should stay optimistic about finding an interested college program but realize if things do not work out, they have done all they could. For those who do not obtain a scholarship, it will be discouraging. Players who still want the opportunity to play despite not landing a scholarship should plan to attend their college of choice's open tryout. It is common for even the top-level college programs to keep a walk-on or two after tryouts. Player's who do not make the team can look into their schools intramural and club programs too.

Love Delayed

Two of my favorite students played college baseball, even though no one would have ever predicted that when they were young. They went about it in very unorthodox ways. One never played organized baseball when young. He was a very good athlete but, for whatever reason, never joined an organized baseball league. He had played ball at home quite a bit through the years, mostly with his dad. When he was sixteen years old, he came into my academy and began taking lessons, and his skills became evident very quickly. He worked hard and tried out for the team his junior year in high school. He made the team, played well the remainder of high school and then played four years of college baseball. Obviously, this is not the recommended way to go about playing college ball. The love of the game was evident in him, and once he decided to put the hard work into it, success came.

The second student was a very good young ballplayer. He had not hit his growth spurt, and he felt burned out after his first year of high school, so he stopped playing. His parents were somewhat perplexed by his decision, because he was talented, but they respected his decision and did not force him to continue. Lo and behold, by senior year, he had grown, but the love of the game did not surface again until sophomore year in college. Not only did his love of the game return, but the motivation to practice returned too. He began practicing his skills again after four years away from the game. His skills returned quickly. He made the college team and started for two years at the collegiate level. As mentioned earlier, when the love of something is present, the motivation to work at it will often follow. The inspiration just came later for this young man.

Stay in Charge

Finally, one thing I always advise young players is to stop playing only when they themselves decide they no longer have the desire to play. Do not let others decide for them when they should stop playing. If a player wants to keep playing and does not make the cut, look for alternatives. Other teams, leagues, levels, schools, or improvement opportunities may present themselves. If every athlete who heard they were not good enough gave up, there would be a whole set of different players at the highest levels.

I doubt anyone who saw me play in high school could have ever predicted that I would play pro ball, let alone make it to the major leagues. When I finished high school, I had no baseball scholarship offers, so I walked on at college and made the team after a tryout. I still had the dream and desire and was going to stop playing only when I felt I was not good enough—not when others told me. Sixteen years later, after a college career, graduation, and professional baseball, I determined for myself that I would hang up the spikes. Players should never give up until they decide it is the time.

The Real Performance Enhancers

Defining Integrity

I ONLY HAD ONE EXPERIENCE with anything associated with performance-enhancing drugs. When the alleged use of performance-enhancing drugs in major league baseball was most prevalent in the late 1990s and early 2000s, a former student of mine who had been a high draft choice came in to see me. He had hit some hard times in the minor leagues with injuries, and he posed this question to me. "Jack, should I try steroids to see if it can help my arm recover and give me a chance at the major leagues again?"

I tried to put myself in his shoes. I remembered how passionate I was to fulfill my dream of playing in the big leagues. From that perspective, I knew it was not an easy decision. I responded that he had to answer that himself and said, "For the rest of your life, you have to look at yourself in the mirror. If you decide to use them and can look in the mirror and live with the fact that you didn't play by the rules, then go ahead." I was glad to see that not long

The Modern Athlete

after our conversation, the young man retired from professional baseball. I was never as proud of a student as I was that day. That young man made a difficult choice. This was a great example of how sports and issues relating to sports challenge players. His character and integrity were on the line, and they came shining through.

Staying in the Baseline

It is almost impossible to talk about sports without the issue of performance-enhancing drugs (steroids, etc.) coming up. It is unfortunate that this is the case, but true. There will always be an issue with these in our society, because we place such a great emphasis on players being the best. In addition, the rewards are so great (millions of dollars and the admiration from many fans), the temptation to use extra means to reach the top will always be an issue.

Parents and coaches should emphasize that achieving full potential is only praiseworthy through hard work, and only through legal means. Studies have shown that young athletes follow what they see the best players doing, so it is up to parents, coaches, and teachers to influence young athletes to do the right thing. Parents have the responsibility of explaining to kids that just because some great athletes use the wrong methods, that does not make it acceptable for them to do it. They can continue to explain that great athletes are people who make mistakes too. Reinforcing what is right and wrong to their kids and expecting them to play within the rules is essential. Putting such high expectations on young athletes that they feel they have to be great to be a success and accepted is not a good practice. Letting kids know you will love and support them no matter how they perform on the field is essential parenting.

Those Were the Days

I believe it may have been easier years ago to stay focused and love playing sports, because there were fewer alternatives. Generally, growing up before the mid-1970s, we had baseball as the activity available in the spring and summer, football in the fall, and basketball for the winter months. Those were the only sports I ever remember watching on TV. If you did not want to be "stuck" with doing chores around the house or having to do homework all the time, you went out and played. Often we concluded that it was much more fun to be outside playing one of those sports. If you could not find a big group to play with, you could usually find a friend or even a sister or brother to play with. It did not have to be an organized practice or game. We would be creative and have some kind of competitive game going even if there were only a couple playing. It just does not happen like that as much anymore.

Since that time, many alternatives have arisen for kids, including many other viable sporting options that were not available years ago. TV has introduced young people to many other sports. What kids see on TV, such as the extreme and other sports, influences them to try those sports. Of course, the biggest change over the years is the video game craze that occupies much of the kids' time. The larger number of alternatives makes it more difficult for kids to want to continue playing a sport when it is not fun. Kids from my generation did not have nearly as many alternatives, so we played the sport of the season or nothing at all.

Additionally, in the past, players learned much of the strategy and skill of the games by playing in unsupervised settings. Nowadays, most playing is in an organized team setting. Because of this, many players today are turned off because of all the supervision and practicing with unqualified coaches. Nowadays, good, creative coaching is essential. Good coaching will determine which sport a player enjoys the most and determines which sport they pursue as they get older. Instructive and fun practices are necessary to keep players excited about the sport. It is a given that the young player will want to pursue the sport they feel is the most fun, and when it is not fun, they have many alternatives to switch to.

Just because a child does not love something and does not practice it does not mean the child should stop playing that activity. That is a decision the parents and child can make. It does mean, though, that parents should lower their expectations of their child's future in that activity. The child's love and work ethic may develop at a later age, but that rarely happens if the parents force the child to play and practice more.

"I Just Want Her or Him to Have Fun"

This is another of the often-stated concerns I would hear from parents when they would bring their son or daughter to my academy. It is an admirable sentiment and expresses what sports should be for young players. Unfortunately, it is not that simple for athletes to "have fun" just because people tell them to. Much goes into having fun, including getting chances to compete, having some success, and being around caring people. Most kids have fun when they begin sports at the very young ages, but it slips away for many when parents and coaches expectations of success and stardom become involved.

Often problems develop, though, when parents and coaches say, "I just want them to have fun," when their actions say otherwise to their kids. Parents say "have fun" after giving them numerous instructions on how to play and place expectations on their performance. Because of this, what many kids hear is that "have fun" first means "do as I say" and "play well," and if you do those things, Mom and Dad will be happy. With this in mind, parents should use the term "have fun" before games and practices without any instructions and individual expectations attached. Players' practice time is the best time for multiple "what to do" instructions. Short-phrase pep talks like "Do your best" or "play hard" before games are ok. The one acceptable expectation parents and coaches should convey to their players is that all players should give as close to 100% as possible.

Climbing Mount Everest

Many parents would ask if I would make their son a major-leaguer. That request always reminded me of the response of a famous athlete when they were asked, "how do I get to the top?" by an up and coming athlete. The famous athlete responded, "If you have to ask, it's not going to happen." The point is, there are no shortcuts. It all starts with love of the game, followed by hard work, which produces success. Those three, love, hard work, and success build upon and feed off each other. No one can make a player a major-leaguer; only the player can do that. Nevertheless, coaches can help players develop a love of sport, a good work ethic, and success. When that results in reaching the top for the player, that is great. When it does not, that is great too, because coaches and parents can be satisfied they taught the performance enhancers of love, hard work, and success. These "natural" performance enhancers have been around forever. When athletes have the three, they will reach their full potential. Coaches and parents are crucial to helping players have all three of the "real performance enhancers."

"All You Need Is Fun"

The first and most important natural performance enhancer is love. People who love something will have fun working on it. Love for sport sometimes just happens, but most of the time, it develops. The best way to develop a love for sport is to have fun playing, and there is no better way of spurring a young athlete to want to work on a sport than to make it fun. We often say "have fun," but without thought as to what fun is. Games are usually fun because of the competition games create, and athletes like to compete. Making practice fun can be a completely different situation, yet it is necessary so athletes will practice and develop the necessary skills. Two of the most common concerns parents have are that their child "doesn't want to work at it" and "they are not having fun." These go hand in hand. When a child does not enjoy a sport, he or she will not want to work at it.

Suggestions for Parents and Coaches to Make Practice Fun:

- ❖ Keep kids active—short instructional talks or displays are better than long, drawn-out speeches. Kids do not care how much you know but want to try what you are teaching them.
- ❖ Present a positive, optimistic, and enthusiastic attitude—this attitude will filter down to the players, and practice will be a happy environment.
- ❖ Offer variety—coaches and parents who can provide different ways (drills, etc.) of working on all aspects of the game—will prevent boredom and maintain exciting practice time.

❖ Offer challenges—athletes are competitive and want challenges—overcoming the challenge, or having the opportunity of overcoming the challenge, is fun.

❖ Little group or individual contests and competitions are great fun as long as everyone has a chance to succeed. Coaches may have to handicap some competitions.

❖ Have a special skills day where every player gets a chance to show his skills is fun. Coaches should do their best to put players in positions where the players will succeed.

❖ Be around teammates who all feel they are an important part of the team is fun.

❖ Giving attention to every player is important. It is difficult for players to have fun if their teammates are not happy.

❖ Fun is success, or at least the feeling of success. Good coaches will recognize good effort and little areas of improvement and will point those out to parents and others. Fun for players is feeling good about themselves and pleasing others (especially their own parents) with their play.

❖ Social interaction among teammates and allowing kids to be themselves is fun. Strict rules and practices when kids do not have time to socialize are a big turnoff for most young players.

❖ Let kids perform other roles during slow times at practice, such as umpiring, coaching, scorekeeping, and announcing, can be fun for players and entertaining for all.

❖ Bring in a guest to talk from time to time is fun. It does not have to be an expert or a big star. For example, a former player from the program or team who has advanced to the high school level is sufficient and memorable to the young athletes.

Hard Work Is the Difference

The great coach John Wooden sums up the second natural performance enhancer:

> Many athletes have tremendous God-given gifts, but they don't focus on the development of those gifts. Who are these individuals? You have never heard of them—and you never will. It is true in sports and it is true everywhere in life. Hard work is the difference—very hard work.

Hard work leads directly to better performances. Good results rarely happen by chance. Hard work, coupled with correct knowledge, is necessary for ultimate success. There is a famous saying that goes "luck is what happens when preparation meets opportunity." Often, people say a player was lucky when they do well or win. In reality, hours and hours of work produced the good results.

The different motivational levels of players determine the amount of work they are willing to do and varies from kid to kid. Very few young players work as hard as they could, but that is probably a good thing. Too much hard work at a young age often leads to burnout. (A detailed discussion about "burnout" will come later.) Parents should promote the idea that hard work leads to success and rarely will success come without the hard work, but they should not push their player to the point of overexertion or disaffection.

Parents can teach a good work ethic to their kids by displaying that in their own lives, at work, and around the house. Generally, kids will understand how to achieve success by what they observe of others. Seeing the success people achieve when they work hard is a great example for kids to follow. Parents might consider taking the kids to work with them occasionally to help set this example of a good work ethic.

Perfect Practice Makes Perfect

People often think professional players show up at seven o'clock for a seven-thirty game, get dressed, and play. They do not realize that the players often arrive three or four hours before game time to work on their skills. I would often tell young players how much work the pro players do every day to impress upon the young players the necessity of hard work and skill repetition. I would tell them about the following announcement by Dave Bristol, a former Milwaukee Brewers manager. He facetiously sums up which players need to practice more: "There'll be two buses leaving the hotel for the park tomorrow. The two o'clock bus will be for those of you who need a little extra work. The empty bus will leave at five o'clock."

There comes a time when adjustments and confidence are necessary, and these will only come with self-knowledge of what one is doing. When parents and coaches provide the knowledge—this will lead to understanding—which will lead to adjustments and confidence. This knowledge and a good work ethic provide players the opportunity to reach their potential and achieve success. Knowledge without the work ethic, or vice versa, will ultimately result in failure and possibly the end of a career. The best preparation is when hard work and knowledge meet.

One of my favorite sayings while teaching over the past twenty years is that it is better to perform a skill ten times correctly than a hundred times incorrectly. "Doing a thing nearly right and doing it exactly right is usually the difference between success and failure" is a famous saying from an unknown source, and suggests the need for correct practice routines.

Many players will work hard at their skills. However, without practicing the correct fundamentals, they are just getting tired and reinforcing bad habits. Looking back on my career, I wish I had learned the fundamentals better, because all too often, I played with little confidence because I did not have a good understanding of the fundamentals. Knowing the fundamentals would have allowed me to focus on correct habits without having to work so hard trying to find the groove repeatedly. Doing fewer repetitions, but more quality repetitions, would have served me better. Coaches and parents should stress quality first. Teaching players to rest when they start to feel tired is good. Otherwise, bad habits may develop out of fatigue. Physical fatigue will lead to mental fatigue, which will lead to uninterested ball players. Notice a player who plays too many games in a row or in a week, and you will recognize what I mean. Quantity is good only if done correctly.

More than once during the 2007 World Series, announcers mentioned Red Sox superstar Manny Ramirez would go in the morning to work on his hitting for the game that night. Although that is kind of unusual, he may be on to something. Although most of the players work hard, his hard work is exemplary—but doing it in the morning and allowing more time for the body and mind to recover before the night game could be a real advantage. Players who do all the work right before the game without much time to recover physically and mentally may be at a disadvantage.

Watching good players perform a skill repeatedly is useful for showing how young people should perform the action themselves, and this can lead to more quality practice time. Young ball players should be encouraged to picture those good players' actions in their own minds. Most behavioral experts will tell you how important this visualization is to improving one's performance. Putting a good fundamental picture in one's mind and then trying to perform that action can help the player's development.

All parents and coaches want their kids to perform well and work hard, but they do not always provide their young players with the know-how to improve. Too often, I see parents and coaches let players get away with bad habits and then get upset when the players do not perform well. Generally, the team coaches know the basics of the game, but it can be difficult to help each individual. The number of players on a team, the time restrictions, and the reality that habits do not change overnight can make it tough for the coaches.

Quality practice time occurs when parents and coaches know the correct fundamentals and can observe when the players are doing them correctly. It is necessary to give players precise instructions on the proper fundamentals. Parents who feel they do not know the fundamentals can obtain this knowledge by reading books, articles, or viewing videos on the fundamentals. The other option is to bring the player to a knowledgeable coach or professional for instruction. Over time, this quality practice will show up with good results, confident players, and happy parents.

Life Champions

The third natural performance enhancer is success, or at least the feel of success. Success and the satisfying attitude that comes with it are great performance enhancers. Self-confidence and self-esteem come with success. Over time, success will be necessary for a player's continual interest in the sport. It is almost impossible to feel like continuing an endeavor when you have no success at it.

Skill development is not always easy, and not everyone can be statistically successful. But this is where good parenting and good coaching can make all the difference. Notice that I mentioned success or at least "the feel of success" as two separate things. Often a player's statistics may not show that he or she is successful, but athletes can still feel successful if they learn the correct definition of success. Beginning at a young age, I recommend that parents explain to their kids that success is working hard and doing one's best, period. In light of what we have seen come out in sports news the last number of years about the commonplace use of performance-enhancing drugs, parents should add that success is only real if done within the rules. Usually, players who work hard and do their best have some success and feel good about themselves, no matter how they performed. On the other hand, athletes who know they did not give their best effort will feel unfulfilled deep down, and their self-esteem suffers, even when they won and performed well.

Often, we allow ourselves as parents, players, and coaches to substitute expectations for success. We expect players and teams to perform a certain way and deem it a failure when they do not. It is up to parents, coaches, and team members to understand the only things a player can control are preparation and effort, and these are what parents and coaches should judge players on. Players are successful when they have prepared and tried their best no matter the score, statistics, and the like. In this atmosphere, a child's self-esteem and self-confidence rise, regardless of the results of their performances.

It is important for parents to make it clear their kids will be considered a success when they prepare and do their best. Eventually, players tend to gravitate toward the endeavors that show the best results from their hard work. Most likely, this will not be a sporting endeavor, as very few can make a living playing a sport, but the work ethic, love, and success learned will benefit them in everything. The following poem by motivational speaker Tom Krause describes the "feeling of success."

Always Be Your Best!

When you think it doesn't matter
if you fail or pass the test
Keep in mind the reason why
you should always be your best.

While the whole world may not notice
if you tried to give your all,
there is a person in you
to whom it matters if you fall.

That little voice inside you—
which directs your thoughts each day—
will make the final judgment
if you won or lost each day.

Never can you fail yourself
if you give it all you've got.
The world extends a hand to you
when you give life your best shot.

For all that really matters
when you're finished with your test,
is not the final score at all
but did you do your best?

— *Tom Krause*
Touching Hearts—Teaching Greatness

Inspiration

Playoff Pitcher

JUST THINK WHAT BASEBALL would have missed if the player in the following story hung up the spikes because he never played? The year was 1980 and I was playing for the Albuquerque Dukes, the Triple A-team for the LA Dodgers. We were in the playoffs for the Pacific Coast League, and as is customary, we were expecting the Dodgers to send us a few players from the Double A-team to help us in our quest for the championship. They sent us one player. He was kind of short and stocky, if not pudgy. We proceeded to lose in the playoffs and the player they sent us never got into a game. I am not sure if our team even knew if he was a pitcher or a position player, but we were not happy. The rest of the winter, we were upset that the Dodgers did not send us anyone that could help, or so we thought.

The following season that player became the talk of major league baseball and went on to become one of the greatest pitchers

In Need of Inspiration

ever. You probably guessed it—in 1981 Fernando Valenzuela and "Fernandomania" was the talk of baseball. We went from being mad at the Dodgers to being mad at our coach because he did not put Fernando in a game in the previous season's playoffs. All joking aside, Fernando did not get upset about not playing and continued working to improve. That is one of the great things about sports—they teach players to get back up when down. Moreover, it certainly helps to have good coaches and parents there to help when players are feeling down.

Lighting the Fire

"He never wants to work at it." It is frustrating for parents when their kids do not want to practice. Often, parents cannot understand this, especially when the parents feel they have been nothing but encouraging with the child's participation in the sport. It is important that parents and coaches understand that they should try to inspire young players, but motivation comes from within the players themselves. All athletes are different. Some are self-motivated at a young age. Others become motivated at a later age, and some never seem to attain the motivation for sports.

Obviously, it is easiest to be the parent of the self-motivated athlete. It can be frustrating to be the parent of the child who does not seem motivated, especially when the youngster appears to have the talent to be good. Parents are in a tough spot. They do not want to push too hard and create tension, but it can be frustrating to see talent wasted. Parents of the child who does not appear motivated should continue to encourage the young athlete and point out that they have talent. Letting your child know, in a non-accusatory manner, that they can develop this talent with desire and practice is good. These words may create the love of the sport and the motivation at some point in a young player's career. For others, the interest level wanes and the love never comes. Sometimes you hear of an athlete who begins a sport at an older age, eleven to thirteen, and becomes successful, but this is rare. When the love of the game is not there at a young age, the interest rarely develops as the player ages.

Even though motivation comes from within the players themselves, parents and coaches can and should provide inspiration at opportune times in players' lives. A dictionary definition of inspiration is "a stimulus to creativity in thought and action." Parents and coaches have a tremendous influence on young players and should not miss opportunities to stimulate thought and action in their kids. There are many ways to inspire and it does not take a great story like Fernando's to inspire kids. Nor is a great speech or gesture necessary. Providing attention, approval, and knowledge helps players acquire the motivation to continue. People can inspire with just a word or two—"awesome" or "great effort"—or with a simple smile at a player who has done something in which you approve.

On the other hand, people often discourage kids by telling them they "can't do something" or they will "never be good enough." Obviously, these are not inspiring comments and should not be said. In addition, showing disgust or ignoring players because they do not want to practice is not a good habit. Probably the most uninspiring tactic is to embarrass a player, especially in front of others.

It's the Day-to-Day Little Things that Count

I have seen many young players whose motivation levels grew in time because their parents were patient and encouraging toward them. Words of praise go a long way toward stimulating young players to continue with an activity. Letting kids know how proud you are of them is vital for their self-esteem and desire to play sports. Of course, it is not good to go overboard with praise, but letting kids know you want them to succeed and you will help them find ways of improving is good. The following are other ways, beyond simply practicing the sport, that inspire young players to improve and become motivated in their day-to-day sports life. These inspiring methods may or may not get players to practice, but they are a way of easing the parent's mind, knowing you are doing all you can do to create a more motivated young player.

What Parent's Can Do:

◈ Watch televised games, or attend games of the particular sport with players; point out how often the top players fail and that it is part of the game. It eases the pressure on young players when they see the best players in the game miss shots, make errors, etc. The greatest athletes like Michael Jordan or Tiger Woods will tell you that behind every great shot there are many failed attempts. Parents can help young players understand this, and like Michael and Tiger, get back up each time with "no fear" of the next attempt and possible failure.

◈ While watching, point out how good players maintain balance, stay focused, and stay fundamentally sound. These little tips will reinforce good habits and make your young player aware of the importance of good fundamentals and focus. Any tip suggested in a positive manner will give the player hope for the next game. Teaching in this non-confrontational way while observing other players is very beneficial, because players feel less threatened in this manner, yet they are still learning.

✧ There are many theories about yelling instructions during the game, but it is important to keep the fundamental instructions to a minimum during the competition. Practice is the recommended time for most instruction. It's difficult to keep quiet during games, because coaches and parents want to help. The problem, though, is twofold. First, it is hard for players to perform and focus fully if they are thinking about what their parents or coach is yelling. Second, players will not learn as quickly or instinctually if they are waiting for you to tell them what to do.

✧ Remind your son or daughter of a good play they had in the past, which will give them a good, positive feeling. This positive picture in their minds will give them the feeling they have done it before and can do it again.

✧ Do not keep the player's statistics, averages, percentages, and the like. These may be good to know when a young-ster is doing well, but they can be very discouraging when performance falls off. It is best to not dwell on numbers and keep the focus on improvement each game. Averages can be very demoralizing when compared to others, and they can give young players the feeling they are a failure. In reality, they may be improving their fundamentals and knowledge, and good results will show up later. Keep reminding them of the long-range goal (making the high-school team, for example), which may be years away. This will give them hope because there is time for improvement, and each game will not have a "do or die" feeling to it.

✧ Have a person whom the player respects talk to the young player about adjustments to their fundamentals. It is comforting to a young player to know the struggles will go away with a fundamental adjustment, as opposed to thinking she or he just is not good enough. This person may be the child's parent, but often it is best coming from another coach or friend.

✧ Watching inspirational sports movies like *Miracle* and *Chariots of Fire* with kids is great. These movies help everyone feel like they can overcome challenges, and they provide a timely pick-me-up for struggling players.

✧ Do not ignore other aspects of the player's game when they are struggling with one part. Point out the importance of other ways to contribute to the team's success. Explaining to them that they can help the team in other ways can balance the hurt they feel. "A great defensive play that saves a score is just as good as a scoring play" is an example.

✧ Helping players keep practice in perspective is also important. Practice is practice, and it is for preparing, warming up, and gaining confidence; but the practice results do not determine the results of the game. Many young players take their negative practice results into the game and are defeated before they even play the game. Likewise, players can put too much stock in a great practice and feel miserable when the game does not go as well as practice. However, explaining to players that practice will pay off soon, or eventually, is good.

✧ When things do not go the player's way, often, the solution is to continue working and even increasing the workload. Sometimes, however, it is best to get the player's mind totally off the negative results. Taking time off and doing things unrelated to the activity can be beneficial. This gives players the opportunity to return to playing with a fresh and determined attitude. Using their best judgment as to whether a child should increase the workload or take time off is the parent's and coach's call. After trying one method without success, they can try the other way the next time.

Not the Most Logical Choice

The following is a speech former major league pitcher Jim Abbott gave to a group of kids, including a little girl who had a handicap similar to Jim's. Jim Abbott was born without one hand yet still played baseball and had a great major league career. Obviously, Jim was one of the most inspirational athletes ever and is now a great motivational speaker. Jim's speech sums up so much about what sports are all about—the passion and love, the benefits of hard work, opportunities and second chances, the role of parents and the celebration of one's successes. Just as watching inspirational movies can help lift a player's spirit, so can telling players stories of great athletes who, like Jim, overcame the odds.

I loved throwing a baseball. It is so important to find something in life you feel crazy about; because you are so passionate, you naturally practice. The hard work it takes to do something well will come easily.

You know how it worked out. I played baseball at the University of Michigan for two United States teams, the 1987 Pan American team and the 1988 United States Olympic team. Even though I played in the major leagues for almost ten years, the Olympics are still one of my favorite memories.

You know in my career, I once won eighteen games in one year. I also lost eighteen games in one year. I was fortunate enough to go straight from the Olympic team to the major leagues, never spending a day in the minors. I was also sent down to the minor leagues after eight years in the big leagues. In 1996, I went 2–18 with a 7-run ERA. I could not get anyone out. I was in the first year of a long-term contract with the team near my home town. It was supposed to be easy. That following year I was fired, drove back to California, crying all the way. I spent that summer up in Michigan hurting and wondering if my career was over. Somewhere deep inside, I was not sure. So, I called the Chicago White Sox for a tryout.

They gave me a chance to pitch again. I would watch the major leagues on TV with the rest of those kids, and it felt like a million miles away. That had been my life. I was away from family whom I know thought I was crazy. Then I got the call, I was going to Chicago back to the show. That was the good news; bad news is you are facing the Yankees Saturday night. They were about 100 and 15 at the time. I went on to win that game against the Yankees that night. In fact, I went 5–0 the rest of that September.

I would like to tell those parents back in my neighborhood how wonderful my own parents were and are. They encouraged me to participate, but did not dwell on every move I made. I do not ever remember a concession to the fact that I had one hand; maybe even a little more was expected. I will always be thankful that they never allowed my hand to be used as an excuse.

I would like to tell that little girl, "Go out and find what it is you love. It may not be the most obvious choice, or the most logical, but never let that stop you." Baseball was hardly the most logical choice for someone with one hand, but I loved it, so that is what I pursued. No matter where the road takes you, do not give up until you know in your heart you have done everything you possibly could to make your dreams come true. You owe nothing to disability, ignore it. When you fail, get back up and try again. Leave no room for an excuse. Do not listen to what you cannot do. Ninety-nine percent of the time, I never think of missing that hand. I have never been envious of someone with two hands. Listen to that voice deep within you; it knows when you have done your best.

Somehow, when things are said and done, there will be some accountability. Imagine someone coming up to you at the end of your life and asking, "You've been given these talents—what did you do with them?" There is a certain potential we owe ourselves to live up to. Work hard, do not look back, and celebrate the blessings in your life.

Unforgettable Memories

Did I Tell You About the Time I . . .

I HAVE READ WHERE AN UNASSISTED triple play
is one of the rarest plays, even more rare than the
perfect game being pitched. I was once involved in a
major league play that may be even rarer than those.
While playing against the Detroit Tigers one day, I
laid a bunt down the third-base line. While I headed
to first base, the pitcher or third baseman picked up
the ball and heaved it past the first baseman. I headed
to second base and saw the third base coach as I
approached the bag. He was waving me on toward
third base, so off I went. As I approached third base,
the right fielder's throw to third went sailing right over
the third baseman's head. Once again, I was off to the
races and scored. Yep, a legitimate "Little-League home

"Who" is on first, but what about? . . .

run." When is the last time you saw that in a major league game? I would like an investigation and a new statistic put in the record books for this achievement. There are tons of "out-of-the-park" homeruns hit every year and plenty of "inside-the-park" home runs, but how many Little-League home runs have you seen at the major-league level? From now on, when people ask me how many home runs I hit in the big leagues, I am going to say two and a half.

Although it was exhausting running that far, it created a great memory. Coaches and parents will have lasting memories of their youngster's playing days. It is those great memories that parents will have and never forget. Those great sports memories will form a bond between parents and kids that will last a lifetime. Ultimately, that may be the best part of sports. Sports create a common interest between parents and kids that will last long after the kids have moved away from home. Whenever my kids call home or I call my parents, we always have sports talk to fall back on when there seems to be nothing else to talk about.

Those memories are one of the parents' rewards for their kids playing sports. The memories, along with the satisfaction of knowing they were there for their kids to teach the life lessons, make the playing days worthwhile. Many of the memories are forgettable, but the memory of that one diving catch, homerun, basket, or touchdown will last a lifetime. Sometimes, the unforgettable memories occur in the car on the way to the games or after games when you stop for a root beer with your son, daughter, or team.

Picture Perfect

Every sport has its memorable, funny moments. As a coach, parent, and fan, I have observed many memorable plays. Often comical, these experiences are "priceless," as the saying goes. I have summed up some of those great memories by each age group below. I am sure you will relate to some of these experiences. I just wish I had a camera for some funniest home video clips. In addition, we'll look at common character traits of kids that are indicative of their age. The following situations and teachings recognize these traits and give the coach suggestions on how to deal with them.

Age Five: Safety First—Yours and Theirs

Clear the runway. Even though your son or daughter is only five years old, you will need a lot of room when playing most sports—stay clear of all breakable objects (windows, cars, pets, other people)—and warn all observers to stand way back. Kids this age are so ready to run, kick, hit, and throw that they have a tendency to act without regard to the surroundings. You may want to post a sign "Play or watch at your own risk." Coaches are responsible for teaching safety for all.

Ready position is not playing in the dirt. The eagerness of this age does not always extend to all players. Kids this age cannot resist the urge to get down and rearrange the dirt during the slow times. Parents and coaches should find ways to make playing the game fun and try to keep players excited about the game.

Age Six: Patience, Coach, Patience

Not that way, it's that way. Most players this age know which direction to go—but they are overcome with the thrill of playing, and they lose all sense of direction. The good news is they love to run at this age and hustle is not a problem. Demonstrating the correct way to do things is beneficial to the players' development.

Play your position. It gets comical when the coach looks out and sees all players standing at the same place. Good coaches assume nothing and point the way for their players.

Age Seven: Rules, Rules

Foul ball—yes, it's a strike, but no, you are not out. Every sport has its confusing rules that young players have to learn. For example, it can be confusing to the young ball player to figure out that every time they hit a foul ball, it is a strike—three strikes and you are out—but a hitter can keep hitting foul balls (which as mentioned are strikes)—and they can keep hitting those foul balls for eternity and they are not out. Huh? What a great game.

That's a force out—no tag needed. Equally confusing to the rising young star is when to tag a player and when just tagging the base is required. The coach is there to teach the rules and strategies of the game.

Age Eight: Practice Makes Perfect

Ouch, good contact—but wait till I get out of the way. This is a great age to begin skill instruction with practice aids, but coach beware. Players get so anxious to show their skills, they start without regard to the coach's whereabouts. Coaches, who are very quick, need to get the heck out of the way (or keep a bag of ice nearby). Use of the three-second rule is good—the young athlete must count to three before beginning to practice—giving the coach time to move.

Don't think, play. Players often want to wait for the coach's instructions before getting involved in the game action. In the meantime, the action has passed them by. Coaches should teach players to not worry about making mistakes, and let them know about those mistakes at a later time.

Age Nine: That's Just Coach Talk

Do as I say, not as I do. Often, coaches try to show players how to perform a skill and then fail miserably. Sometimes, coaches forget how difficult it is to do things and embarrass themselves in front of their players.

Stealing is allowed. The coach may have to explain that some terms in sports are not to be taken literally, and players will not get in trouble if they do it.

Age Ten: Frustration and Pressure

There's no crying. The competition level improves dramatically at this age, so the frustration level also increases. The skills required for success are difficult to master. Sports are often games of failure, where even the greatest players in the world fail. Explaining to the future star that failure is part of the game is important. Self-pressure is common and may lead to crying, but excessive parent or coach pressure is always unacceptable.

Stay focused on the game; you don't have to look in the stands after every play. Likewise, the pressure factor increases at this level. Emphasizing to the young star that just competing, having fun, and continuing to work hard are what is important, and they do not have to look for approval from Mom and Dad during the game.

Age Eleven: Coach Is the Coach

Peyton Manning is a professional—when you get there, you can play that way, but for now do it the way I tell you. Kids this age will have discovered *Sportscenter*, where every play is spectacular and worth trying. They will begin to copy the habits of the great players, thinking that style looks "cool." Coaches can explain to the young superstar that it is best to keep things simple and success will follow. Allowing kids to experiment with different styles is ok, but remind them there are always good fundamentals behind the style.

Listen to me, not your friend Johnny. I suggest that coaches remind players that you, the coach, know more than their friend knows, and you are there to help.

Age Twelve: Reality Sets In for Players

That's the way the ball bounces. Just when players think they have it all figured out, the size of the players greatly increases. This can be overwhelming for some, especially the small player. Coaches might like to explain to the young player that good fundamentals and practice are necessary to improvement.

I did not say a dirty word. Up until this age, the best players usually play the "action" positions. At this age, some of the best players will have to realize there are better players for their position, and they must try an alternate one. Coaches may have to explain to the young player there is no shame in playing a less glamorous position, and often the best athletes play those other positions.

Age Thirteen: Reality Sets In for Parents

It's not funny when you hit me with the ball. Often players' ability levels have surpassed Mom and Dad's ability to keep up. Parents and coaches who try to keep up must accept the consequences and may be embarrassed from time to time. Even though being hit by the ball is never fun, often the observer's first reaction is to laugh. Players can explain to their parents that they are stronger now, and those parents who want to continue practicing with their players should use protective gear to stay healthy.

Be quiet, Mom and Dad. Oh, the change of life (puberty) has started. Mom and Dad no longer have the influence they once did. Players do not want them yelling to them at games or hanging around them too much around their friends and teammates, either.

Age Fourteen: Patience, Parents, Patience

Even though you think your coach sucks, do what he tells you. Oh, the teenage years! The greatest kid in the world will all of a sudden look at the coach with a blank stare and wonder, What planet is the coach from? The coach realizes it is going to be a long summer when his best jokes get no response whatsoever. Parents may have to communicate to their kids that even though you know they (the kids) know everything, their coach might not know it and so they should pay attention to the coach.

They really do care. Likewise, the coach will be wondering why he volunteered for such an uncaring group. It is the age, Coach. The key is to keep instructing in a civil way, avoid the screaming when they make mistakes, and do not give up on them. Coaches have no reason to panic. The fun-loving kid usually returns in a year or so.

Age Fifteen: Teamwork

The balls don't pick themselves up. Kids still playing at this age are generally age committed, but they see it as important to "be cool" and not hustle too much and show up the other players. Kids love to play but picking equipment up in a reasonable period may be a problem. Coaches should explain the meaning of "team" and what it means to help each other.

We should have won. Players this age always feel like they are the better team, which is fine. However, coaches may need to keep reminding them that the better team that day did win, and improvement and the elimination of mistakes are necessary to win the next game.

Age Sixteen: TV's Influence

He did not hit you on purpose. TV plays a big role with the impressionable young ball player. Bench-clearing brawls and similar unsportsmanlike conduct have no place in youth sports. At this age, players want to prove how tough they are and start to question the opposing team's motives. Coaches might like to inform the "tough guy" that rough play is part of the game, so they should hustle and try not to rub the sore spot. It is always best to let the opposing player know the contact did not even hurt. (Great acting skills may be required).

Only pros do not hustle all the time; the rules state that high-school players have to. A little fibbing (just kidding) may be in order to keep kids hustling. Nothing looks worse than seeing a player "dog it" and not play hard. Suggest to players that they owe it to themselves and their teammates to give 100% at all times.

Age Seventeen: Patience, Players, Patience

The game is on the field, people. Cars and the opposite sex are now important to the distracted athlete. Divulging to the players that they need to stay focused while on the field is a constant duty of the coach. Explaining that they owe it to themselves to "reach for their potential" and the cars and girls and guys will be there after the game is another goal of the coach.

Teamwork, everyone, teamwork. There is good reason to remind players that being the game's star is ok, but teams win games with offensive execution, defense, and togetherness.

This is not a true story. At least I do not think it is, but as former major-league pitcher, Joaquin Andujar once said, "There is one word in America that says it all about baseball: youneverknow." It is another of the great stories whose author is unknown.

The Fish That Got Away

It was the day of the biggest game of the year. Scouts, fans, and everyone who was anyone came that day. Not only were they coming to see two great teams; they were also excited to see one of the best players to come along in awhile. Hackin' Hal was his name. When Hackin' came up to bat in the third inning, his team was trailing 1 to 0. Hackin' Hal was a switch-hitter. Batting left-handed to face the right-handed pitcher, he proceeded to blast one out of the park to tie the score. When Hackin' came up in the sixth inning with his team trailing 2 to 1, he did the same thing and tied the score with a long homerun.

The game remained tied, 2–2 into the ninth inning when Hackin' came to the plate. Everyone there was on the edge of their seats, wondering if Hackin' Hal would untie the score. They were not disappointed, but just how he did it was a surprise.

This time he was batting right-handed, facing a left-handed pitcher. Hackin' hit a shot into the right center field gap. It was at this moment that Hackin' became a little confused and started running, but running toward third base and not first. The third base coach was putting his arms up and screaming at Hackin' to turn around, but Hackin' paid no attention as he rounded third base and headed for second. The ball was still being tracked down, so Hackin' headed for first. By this time, the first-base coach realized it was too late, so he waved Hackin' home. The ball came, Hackin' slid, and amid a cloud of dust, the umpire yelled safe.

Well, that untied the game. A run was taken away from Hackin's team for the reverse homerun, and the score reverted to 2 to 1. Hackin's team lost. It was never confirmed, but it was rumored that Hackin' Hal never put the spikes on again.

6

Keeping the Fire Under Control– Avoiding Burnout

Enjoying the Ride

"Playing in the major leagues was a 'dream come true' experience for me. When I look back, though, the fun part was the journey getting to that level. The work put into it, the day-to-day challenges, the friendships made, and the striving for the goal were the most exciting things. Every young player a coach comes across has dreams, whatever those dreams may be. The coach and the game can provide the means to understand how to reach those dreams. By teaching players the work ethic necessary to be successful and helping them meet the challenges the game presents, helps mold their future. Furthermore, being a friend and a role model will help them throughout their journeys."

—Jack Perconte (The Making of a Hitter)

Where there's smoke, . . .

I HAVE SEEN IT ALL TOO OFTEN, players, parents, or coaches become so goal oriented they forget to enjoy each and every day. It is great to have goals and work toward them, but it often leads to a dead-end when the focus on the goal takes the fun out of the journey. All involved should be sure they recognize it is the experience along the way that is important, and not the goal itself. I always felt like getting to the major leagues was my goal, although it was also a means to an end. I did not know what the end was at the time, but I knew that it was out there and working toward a goal would pay off in one way or another. People who do not understand that it is the journey and the fun that is important, often leave the sport with bitterness.

Former major league pitcher and author, Jim Bouton, once wrote in his book *Ball Four,* "A ballplayer spends a good piece of his life gripping a baseball, and in the end it turns out it was the other way around all the time." Often this is true, where the process overtakes players without anyone realizing it. "Burnout" frequently happens to athletes but can also affect many other areas of life as well. It is a concept that is often associated with athletics because the drive for excellence can be addictive. Over the years, "burnout" has evolved into a catchall word for the reason why athletes stop playing. In reality, most athletes' playing days end for other reasons including:

1. Lack of success—when the player feels like the results are not worth the effort exerted
2. The interest no longer exists—other endeavors have taken over
3. Friends stop playing—player's closest friends are doing other things and player does not want to be away from them.

The Flame is Getting Too Hot

Burnout occurs when an activity stops being fun for the athlete. The athlete who burns out is usually still successful; deep down they love the sport and their friends still play. The enjoyment of playing has slipped away because of extensive play under stress. This is a shame because some very talented athletes dropped out when their careers did not have to end that way. In fact, burned-out players were often the most dedicated players and team leaders. Recognizing and addressing the initial signs of burnout, however, is essential in preventing it. Athletes who burn out usually do not return to the sport, although in some rare cases they do.

The cause of burnout is frequently linked to stress caused by parents and coaches. On the other hand, some athletes are very driven and push themselves too hard. This attitude of determination is a characteristic we admire in our athletes and rightly so. However, sometimes athletes become so determined that it turns into an obsession. This obsession with an activity leads players to work so hard they eventually lose the joy of doing it anymore. The other burnout situation that occurs involves a player and a driven parent or coach. Some parents and coaches ride a player so hard that eventually the player's enjoyment of playing disappears. It is important for people to recognize the early signs of burnout so that measures are taken to try to reverse the spiral toward it.

Signs that Burnout May Be Setting in for an Athlete

Athlete now	Athlete in previous years
Not happy even after performing well	Happy and smiling after playing
Does not want to practice or go to team practice	Looked forward to practicing
Does not listen to parent or coach	Used to listen and try suggestions
Ignores or shows disdain for team rules	One of the team leaders
Appears stressed and gets angry easily	Kept emotions under control
Has trouble staying focused	Always had their head "in the game"
Seems restless and may have trouble eating and/or sleeping	Sleep was no problem
Takes losses personally as if it is their fault	Kept losses in perspective

Suggestions for Parents and Coaches to Help Prevent Burnout in Athletes:

✧ Show balance in their own lives where not everything revolves around the sport and their child in that sport.

✧ Do not run from activity to activity without rest periods. Keep a balanced, daily schedule.

✧ Players should play only one sport per season, (fall—football, for example).

✧ Stress the importance of playing for fun, not to please others, but to enjoy play for self.

✧ Recognize the positives in player's performance before offering constructive advice.

✧ Keep realistic goals; anything attained beyond those goals is a bonus.

✧ Set long-range goals and do not dwell on each game.

✧ Do not use conditioning as punishment.

✧ Look for camps, clinics, programs, and coaches that stress the fun of playing and learning.

✧ Instead of forcing players to practice or play, encourage them to do it.

✧ Only play travel ball with one sport, especially if the seasons overlap at all. (See Chapter 10 for a further discussion of travel ball.)

✧ Stress the importance of other interests outside of sports, especially hanging out with friends.

✧ Have player tryout for teams that have coaches who care for the player's well being and growth even beyond the playing field.

✧ Do not allow athletes to get physically run down very often and make sure rest periods and days off are built into the program.

✧ Play fewer games by setting aside one weekend a month free from games.

✧ One to three days of each week should be sport free during the season, depending on age (for younger children schedule more days off).

✧ Limit months of play with no more than nine months of sport-specific practice.

Suggestions for number of months to play one sport:

- ✧ Under thirteen years old—four months of competition (games), two extra months of practice
- ✧ Thirteen and fourteen- year-olds—five months of competition (games), 2–3 extra months of practice
- ✧ High-school age—five months of competition (games), four months of extra practice

Push, Nudge, or Hands-Free

One cannot talk about burnout without mentioning the pushing of an athlete. This is another of those common sports terms that many talk about, but its definition is elusive. "Pushing" is when a player, parent, or coach becomes obsessed with an activity for the player, to the exclusion of almost everything else.

Some athletes push themselves too hard. They often have obsessive personalities and although their work ethic is admirable, their parents and coaches should try to encourage them to "slow down." Otherwise, the result may be a burned-out athlete down the road.

Other athletes are pushed too hard by others, most often a parent or an influential coach. When players are pushed too hard by others, it usually leads to burnout and hurt feelings. It is important to identify the signs of an athlete being pushed too hard and approaching burnout.

Signs that Parents or Coaches are Pushing Too Hard:

✧ Making threatening comments like "I'm not going to pay for this if that is what you are going to do," "I'm not coming if that is how you are going to play," or "You have to practice or else." Then there are comments similar to these that are even worse, "You stink" or "I can't believe how bad you played."

✧ Having the player practice or play so much that the player gets emotionally and physically drained.

✧ Ignoring son or daughter because of their performance.

✧ Mentioning in front of others how bad he or she (the player) is playing.

✧ Never giving the player rest days or days away from sports.

✧ Making players push through injuries and not letting players heal first.

✧ Not allowing other activities at all—especially things with other friends—or limiting outside activities until they practice the sport first.

✧ Never being satisfied with player's performance.

✧ Having the player specialize at too young an age (around twelve and under).

✧ Over-scheduling kid's organized activities.

✧ Seems like the only thing you ever do with the child is play or talk about the sport.

✧ Child is always looking in stands for approval from mom or dad. (May just be a sign of nerves too.)

Another Great Perspective

The following is a famous poem whose message parents should remember the next time they get upset at a youth game or with a young athlete.

He is Just A Little Boy

He stands at the plate,
with his heart pounding fast.
The bases are loaded,
the die has been cast.

Mom and Dad cannot help him,
he stands all alone.
A hit at this moment,
would send the team home.

The ball meets the plate,
he swings and he misses.
There's a groan from the crowd,
with some boos and some hisses.

A thoughtless voice cries,
strike out the bum.
Tears fill his eyes,
the game's no longer fun.

So open your heart
and give him a break.
For it's moments like this,
a man you can make.

Please keep this in mind,
when you hear someone forget.
He is just a little boy,
and not a man yet.

— *Chaplain Bob Fox*

7

Coaches Should Be from Heaven, not H * * *

Understanding Coach-Speak

I was beginning to wonder what I had gotten myself into when I first began my pro career. After signing a pro contract, I was sent to Lodi, California (Dodgers A-ball team) because the team needed a second baseman. Upon arriving, I was told the team currently had four second basemen and I was the fifth. Ok. Having arrived too late to suit up for that night's game, I watched as the team proceeded to lose 20–4. Post-game, our coach came into the clubhouse, closed all the doors and really let the team have it. He yelled, swore, threatened changes and had me shaking in my shoes and wondering if this was normal for professional baseball. He was "hot under the collar" as they say, and screamed words that I had never heard before while degrading the team's play. "Welcome to pro ball," the trainer said to me on the way out the door.

Patience is a virtue

My situation improved quickly. The following day, the Dodgers released two of the second basemen; they sent one down to the lower level and the other became a utility player. I was the starting second baseman, living the dream and the owner of a few new words that I never knew existed. I realized this was not college ball anymore. It was a business where you are only as good as your last game. I noticed that people took this very seriously and players either produce or are moved out.

IT IS IMPORTANT TO UNDERSTAND that professional sports and amateur athletics are two different entities and should have very different perspectives. One thing that does not change is that sports are very competitive and it is "survival of the fittest." It may not seem that way at the lower levels of youth sports, but eventually it will become that way. Athletes who are good enough move on to the next level and the rest find other endeavors to pursue. Often, the coach is the one who has to make the difficult decision of who moves on and who does not. It is rarely fun for the coach to have to make these choices. Parents and coaches should try to empathize with the deciding coach's unenviable position. Although it's natural for some parents and players to be upset, speaking ill about the coach is inappropriate.

I have been fortunate to come across many great coaches in my career. Along with my family, they have shaped my life and were a big reason for the successes I achieved. However, there were many times I did not agree with the decisions of my coaches, thinking them to be wrong or inconsequential. After a while, I recognized the significance of their decisions and the lessons they taught. Luckily, I believe most of those things were for the good in my life. Whether a player has a long career or a short one, I hope they have come across a coach, or many, who makes a difference for the good in their life.

Love-Hate Relationships

The number one reason for complaints by parents whose children play sports (besides maybe "the umpire stinks") is probably directed toward the coach. It is often said about the coach: "He doesn't know what he's doing," "She is only coaching so her daughter can play," "The coach is not being fair to my son," or "He is always on my kid's back." Often the complaints come from players and parents of players who are not performing very well. They do not want to take responsibility for the player's poor play and blame the coach for their inferior play. If one were to poll team members about the performance of the coach, the players answers would tell you a lot about who plays and who does not. Players who play most of the time "like" the coach, and players who do not play much "dislike" the coach.

My first thought when I hear one of these complaints is "have you ever coached before?" It is not as easy as it looks. Coaching is a difficult job because they have to keep everybody, from players, parents, and league officials, happy. As the level of play increases and as winning becomes a bigger issue, the difficulty and pressure for the coach increases.

Just like great athletes, coaches do not just wake up one day as great coaches. They use much trial and error and endless experiences to arrive at teaching, and leadership techniques that work to help players improve. Coaches of young players (pre-high school) often do not have the experience level to be great coaches or the experience to please everyone.

What Parents Can Expect

Placing unreasonable expectations on a child's volunteer coach serves no purpose. However, parents and leagues can expect two things from coaches. First, they can expect that coaches have at least a basic understanding of the game, which allows them to teach enough of the fundamentals and game knowledge for players to improve. Second, they can expect that coaches help every player on the team—not just their own son or daughter or the star players. A good coach sees that players get equal attention from the coaching staff.

Parents should understand that the coaches are there to teach the game to the best of their ability. The ideal situation is when players have a coach who creates a friendly and fun environment, but there is no guarantee of this. As long as the coach is not abusive in any way, the player and parents will probably have to accept the coach with his or her faults, hope the coach cares for the players, and hope their child is improving and learning. Not all coaches will have great people skills, but that does not mean they are inadequate to be a coach. They may be a little rough around the edges but are in no way abusive. These coaches simply do not have the ability or experience to make the game fun, yet they mean well. Additionally, it is a bonus if the coach teaches other life lessons. Although the teaching of life lessons is truly a responsibility of parents, sometimes parents may be lucky to have the help of a good coach. (A discussion of many of these life-teaching moments comes later in this book.)

The Ultimate Coach Quiz

> No written word or spoken plea can teach
> our youth what they should be,
> Nor all the books on all the shelves
> For it is what the teachers are themselves.
> *in Wooden & Jamison, 1997—Original author unknown*

The best coaches and parents lead by example. When adults display integrity and class in their everyday lives and on the playing fields, they create invaluable role models for the young athletes. Good coaches have the ability to develop solid relationships with their players. Coaches who can build good relationships with their players also have a much better chance of being able to relate to their players and offer constructive criticism, without creating tension with their players.

Coaches should never stop working at developing relationships, learning the game, and being positive influences for young people. With this in mind, below is a checklist of the essential attributes that make up a great coach.

Coaches can take the following quiz to see
1. If they are qualified to coach.
2. Where they are on the coaching scale.
3. Where they can improve as a coach.

Parents can analyze a coach's ability by taking the following quiz with their opinion of their child's coach in mind. (The scoring scale for the quiz is located on page 98.)

Responsibilities—Please check all that apply.

1. I am committed to help each player on the team equally, not just my son, daughter or favorite players.
2. I am determined to be fair with playing time and discipline. I will keep a chart of playing time for each player and explain team rules in writing.
3. I am confident that my experience and knowledge of the sport is adequate for the level I am coaching.
4. I continue to further my knowledge of the sport by attending coaching clinics, reading books, watching videos, etc., and become certified, if required, by league.
5. I hold a pre-season meeting with parents to discuss the team's objectives, coaching philosophy, and parental concerns. I expect parents to be there and bring their concerns.
6. I live up to the coaching philosophy throughout the season as stated in the preseason meeting, and attempt to find assistant coaches who share a similar philosophy.
7. I am aware of safety issues common to the sport and always keep in mind the child's health first.
8. I play to win, with the understanding that player development and fun are of equal importance.
9. I challenge each player according to their ability level, in order to help them reach their potential, and provide sports-related practice homework after workouts.

Patience—Please check all that apply.

10. I understand that just because a skill is easy for some or appears easy from the sidelines, does not mean it is easy for everyone.

11. I realize habits are hard to break and just because I tell an athlete what is wrong, that does not mean they can automatically change the habit.

12. I use two voices—a matter-of-fact voice when dispensing information and when players do not seem to be catching on, and an excited voice when they seem to be "getting it."

13. I treat my own child the same as other team members—no more emotion than shown to the rest of the team.

14. I do my best to recognize the difference between effort and results and between physical and mental mistakes. I will teach when mental mistakes are made and encourage when physical ones are made. I will praise effort and be understanding of results.

Self-Expectations—Please check all that apply.

15. My goal is to have my team better at the end of the season than at the beginning.

16. My goal is that every player on the team wants to continue playing the following year.

17. I make the game as fun as possible for the players.

18. I do not under-coach my team nor over-coach my team. Under-coaching is the practice of withholding pertinent game or skill information from a player or team for whatever reason. Over-coaching is yelling out "what-to-do" information as the game action is occurring. Players should make their own decisions. Good coaches let the players play and instruct before and after plays, especially at practice.

19. I do my best to incorporate individual skill work with game strategy to further the knowledge of my players.

Enthusiasm—Please check all that apply.

20. I look forward to practice time as much or more than I look forward to games. Practice is my time to shine and it is the time to put my knowledge of the game into practice.

21. My actions and effort at practices and games show I want to be there with the team and the things I am teaching will have lasting importance for the team.

22. I realize that enthusiasm is contagious—if I display it, it will carry over to my team, parents, and organization. Having a whole team of enthusiastic players is my goal.

23. I am prepared and organized for practices, using every minute for productive work.

Self-Esteem Building—Please check all that apply.

24. I do my best to understand each player's personality so I can determine how to make them feel good about themselves and their play.

25. I recognize the contribution made by each player, no matter how small the contribution.

26. I mention positive player effort and improvement to the players' parents when possible. I understand parents appreciate nothing more than knowing their child is working hard and showing improvement.

27. I know how much a smile, a pat on the back, and words of encouragement can mean to a young player.

28. I look for the signs of players who lack or are losing confidence and try to help build their confidence.

29. I do not tear down the team or any player with negative words or body language.

30. I do not accept the idea that a player is beyond hope—no player, who wants to work at it, is beyond hope and my help.
31. Players may lose confidence, but I will do my best not to lose confidence in them and continue to find situations where they can be successful.
32. I never ignore a player, including my own son or daughter, because of their poor performance on the field. I do not ignore players, even if they get mad when I try to help.

Consistency—Please check all that apply.

33. I consistently teach and lead up to my ability level.
34. I do not let the little things slide—if the timing is not right for teaching, I save it for a later time.
35. I understand sports require repetition and more repetition to develop consistent and instinctive players.
36. I keep the instruction as simple as possible, always sticking with good fundamentals and understanding that fundamentals are fundamentals for a reason—they work.
37. I will stay focused during the game and apply the tactical strategy that I feel necessary.

Perspective—Please check all that apply.

38. I will never forget the age of my team and never have a player play a position they are uncomfortable with.
39. If tryouts that involve cuts are necessary, I am objective in my decisions. I have compassion for the players I have to let go. I try to find a way to keep all players if only one or two extra players are trying out.
40. I keep my cool when: players lose their temper, parents get upset, umpire blows a call, games get tense, or we lose the game.

41. I demonstrate and teach sportsmanship and develop leaders to the best of my ability.

42. I choose to be a positive role model for my players, the parents, school, and organization.

43. I do my best to provide constructive criticism of a player's actions and not direct it at the person.

44. I will teach the importance of "team" and never blame a player or players for a loss. Teams win and lose as a team.

45. I understand the games are for the players and it is their time to shine, not my time to put on a show.

Communication—Please check all that apply.

46. I will keep the lines of communication open between coaches, parents, and league.

47. Communication and input from players is important—I keep players informed of expectations, roles, and coaching decisions affecting them when deemed appropriate.

48. I do what seems best for the team, always being receptive to the thoughts and ideas of others.

49. When it comes time to criticize and "come down" on the team, I do not ridicule players lack of production and stay focused on things they can control—effort. Likewise, I do not "show up" an individual at any time. "Showing up" a player is the act of calling out an individual in front of others with the purpose of putting them in a negative situation.

50. I will do my best to recognize when it is time to inspire the team and individuals and when it is time to back off and use humor to relax them.

Scoring Scale

5 points for statements 1, 7, 13, 22, 27, 29, 39, 40, 42, and 44
2 points for statements 4, 6, 8, 14, 16, 17, 24, 32, 45, and 49
1 point for all other statements

Coaching Rank

92–100 = Great Coach—parents should be so lucky to come across such a coach
82–91 = Good Coach—very adequate
70–80 = Acceptable at lower levels
Under 70 = Needs Improvement—probably should not be coaching or needs a great amount of improvement

Becoming a great coach involves a great deal as evidenced by the amount of ingredients that were involved in the above checklist. Parents should understand the level of commitment and experience involved for a coach to be everything they want them to be. Coaches can improve. Great players are made; great coaches are made too.

Parent's Responsibility Toward the Coach Checklist.

All points checked are worth 25 points. 100 points is necessary to reach full potential as an athlete's parent.

1. As long as my child's coach is not abusive in any way, I will respect him or her and the decisions they make. I will give the coach credit when it is due and thank them for coaching.

2. I will only confront the coach if my child is coming home after games and practices distraught with how things are going with the team or coach. I will approach the coach

in a polite way, determined to work things out so my kid's attitude can improve.

3. I will not bad-mouth the coach, especially in front of my son or daughter and will encourage them to respect their coach.

4. I will not have unrealistic expectations of the coach and promise to volunteer the following season if I feel I am qualified and can do better.

Are You Free for Lunch?

It only takes one unhappy parent to turn the season into a very long one for the coach. Often this unhappy parent will look for allies with some of the other parents and they will let their kid know they are not satisfied with the coach. Things between the coach, team, and parents can deteriorate very quickly and then there are major problems. The negative attitude could have been prevented if the coach could have "nipped it in the bud" when it started with the initial parent. The coach can do a few things. First, at the recommended pre-season meeting, the coach must state his coaching philosophy and discuss any concerns or issues the parents have. Discuss is the important word in that sentence. Second, the coach must live up to the philosophy stated throughout the season. Third, the coach should talk to the parent who appears unhappy as soon as possible in a casual way. For example, when the parent comes to pick up his or her child after practice, start up a conversation like, "Looks as if you came from work, what do you do for a living?" Then proceed from there and try to find some common interests or friends with the parent. Have a casual conversation about things unrelated to the sport at hand. Once the parent notices that you are a nice person with interests beyond the playing field, they will have a much more difficult time bad-mouthing you and your coaching style. Even better, after a few casual conversations, the upset parent may feel like they can now approach you about their concerns, and disagreements can be worked out before the situation worsens.

It's Just a Matter of Trust

As mentioned, coaches cannot get away with any sort of abusive behavior that may have been somewhat acceptable years ago. One inappropriate comment or action by the coach will often lead to their dismissal. With this in mind, coaches must have patience and understanding to earn the trust of their players. Without this trust, players will become disinterested, disenchanted, and they will move on to another sport. It only takes one disruptive player to make the season miserable for the coach. Patience and understanding are especially necessary when dealing with the disruptive player. Over time, coaches can gain the trust of their players when they adhere to the following basics:

- ❖ "How?" to say things—teaching players with an informative tone and not a demeaning one is a sign of a good coach. Always open with something positive before letting the player know what needs to be changed. For example, "I liked the way you did such and such, now let's try this." Good coaches also involve players' input by asking questions like, "Can you tell me why you are doing it like that?" This creates a "we" feeling between the player and coach.

- ❖ "When?" they coach—teaching at the most opportune time is helpful. This is not always immediate because there are times when it may be best to wait to teach. Allowing a mistake or two during warm-ups will give the attitude that you do not expect perfection (immediately, anyway).

✧ "Why?" they want players to do something a particular way—coaches gain credibility with players when they can explain clearly and simply why players should do something a certain way.

✧ "What?" to teach is obviously of importance. Of course, coaches should have the basic knowledge of the sport so players can improve.

✧ "Where" to teach—at practice, before and after games is best. Teaching during games should focus on strategy and tactics, as opposed to skill training.

✧ "Who?" to teach—previously mentioned, but worth repeating, coaches should teach all players, not just the ones they like. The whole team will notice that and they will respect the coach because he/she does not neglect any player. (Neglect or ridicule toward any player on the team may negatively affect each player on the team.)

The Heart to Heart

There comes a time in every coach's career when they do not see eye to eye with one or more of the players on the team. When the situation lingers, a one-on-one meeting with the player or each player may be necessary. The coach should prepare before the meeting, with the intention of having a fruitful meeting where both sides will have a better understanding afterward. It is not wise to hold the meeting immediately after an intense game or practice. Meeting with the player at a more tranquil time, like an off day, is best. Additionally, if the coach feels like the player may get upset, violent, or misconstrue what the coach is saying, it is advisable that the coach has an assistant sit in on the meeting. The best course of action is for the coach to ask questions and listen intently to the player's concerns, before giving his/her side of the situation. More often than not, this "clear the air" meeting leads to a greater understanding and better long-term relationship between the two. It is important that the coach does not say things that will further alienate the player. At the same time, the coach must remain fair and uncompromising in doing what is best for the team.

Your Seat is Right Over There

Coach John Wooden said that maybe his best teaching tool was the bench. Good coaches know how to use the bench or benching a player to make a point, or to motivate their players when necessary. The benching of players "should not" be part of the game for young players and recreational leagues. However, as players age and the caliber of ball improves, the bench can serve a purpose for the coach. Using the bench to get players to give more effort, listen, or behave are all acceptable means to encourage and inspire players.

Dealing with the sometimes-fragile feelings of the player and player's parents can be a delicate area for the coach. Good coaches have concrete reasons for benching a player and are prepared to explain these reasons to the player and parents if need be. Good coaches do not use the bench for vindictive reasons, but for the good of the player and team.

Additionally, using the bench for young players over poor performance, when their effort was good, is not a good practice. Using the bench to give a player a rest is acceptable, of course.

The following is a story from a friend, Ann Duncan, that exemplifies a great use of the bench.

Benched Parents

This select travel team was full of very dedicated players who had everything going for it except one thing. The parents of the players were very outspoken and unruly at the team's games. They yelled at everyone, including their own team, the other team, and the officials. The coach held meetings with the parents and explained it was detrimental to the team and embarrassing for him as the coach, but things did not change. Finally, the coach had an idea. He gathered all the parents and told them that from now on, for any parent who yelled anything but positive statements, their child would sit on the bench for the remainder of the game. If a parent did not like the new rule, they could take their kid off the team. The "benching of the parents," so to speak, worked and the season went along much more smoothly for all. Of course, it helped that the coach was a well-respected coach and many parents wanted their kid to play on his team. Most importantly, is the example of how a coach used the bench as a teaching tool for life lessons for parents as well as players.

Benched Coaches

We often talk of players who become burned out, yet fail to recognize coaches can suffer from the same thing. Often, the coach is the only one who knows when they feel burned out. Many of the same signs of burnout discussed previously for players apply to coaches as well. Most coaches love the sport and the competition, but over time, their enthusiasm for the game wanes. Signs of this lack of enthusiasm often show up in practice in a number of ways including, teaching the first fifteen minutes of practice then shutting it down or letting slide many fundamental and tactical mistakes by their team. The biggest tell-tale sign of coaching burnout is when the coach stops wanting to make a positive difference in their players lives and careers. Coaches and assistant coaches should keep an eye out for each other to help when the rigors of coaching seem to be making inroads on the coach's personality. Usually, only the coaches themselves can admit to burnout, but when it occurs, they should try to remind themselves why they got into coaching in the first place. If they lost this feeling, they should consider taking a break from coaching.

Teaching Confidence, Building Optimism

Motivation from an Unlikely Source

One thing I did not realize when I made it to the major leagues was that umpires were also good hitting coaches. This realization came to me in one of my first games with the Los Angeles Dodgers. Late in a game one night in Atlanta, Tommy Lasorda sent me in to pinch hit with two men on base. The first pitch appeared outside to me and, as was my habit, I followed the ball all the way into the catcher's glove with my eyes and then naturally looked up at the umpire. "Strike," he barked. The next pitch was the same thing, with my eyes going to the umpire as I took the next pitch too. "Strike," he yelled again. It was at this point that "coach" umpire took over. "Hey rookie, you better swing the bat and stop looking at me or you will be back on the bench before you can blink." Needless to say, I would be swinging at the next pitch if it was anywhere in the stadium, and that is exactly

Optimism Is Good, But Don't Forget Reality

what I did. Being a little (ok very) nervous, I swung early on the next pitch but was fortunate to hook the ball down the right-field line for a game winning triple. Thank you, Mr. Umpire. I learned a couple of valuable lessons that night. One, a lesson I knew but almost forgot, was it is very difficult to get a hit if you do not swing and, two, do not look at the umpire if you are a rookie.

"He/She Won't Listen to Me"

THIS IS ANOTHER ONE OF THE COMMON concerns parents would tell me, and something that would cause frustration for the parents. They just could not understand why their kid would not take their sports advice. There can be any number of reasons why kids develop this "be quiet, mom/dad" attitude when their parents would offer helpful advice. More often than not, parents speak in a very emotional voice when giving instructions and this puts undo stress on the young player. This emotional voice is common because parents care so much and want to help so badly. Unfortunately, the emotion the parent puts into their voice places pressure on the child so that, over time, their kids tell them to be quiet, or they tune them out altogether. Parents that can keep the emotion out of their voices when dispensing instructions have the best chance of getting their kids to pay attention to their sports advice.

Other times, players may feel their parents "don't know what they are talking about." This may or may not be true, even if the parent feels like they do know the game. Demonstrating the correct way to do things, instead of telling kids what to do, or showing them the correct way through video or pictures can alleviate the situation.

Finally, it may be that the player simply wants to establish their independence from his parents and show them that they can do something on their own and without mom and dad's help. This attitude is understandable and admirable and parents should try to recognize this is the case and not take it personally.

Rough Day, But It's All Good

Another common concern parents have is that their child has no confidence. Often, they would ask me to help build up their child's confidence. Of course, I would work on that because that is what good coaches do. Of more importance, I felt, was to make sure the young players had an overall optimistic outlook. Confidence is great, optimism is even better. Just like people in general, some athletes are naturally confident, whereas others have no confidence. Players also have different confidence levels, ranging from very confident to somewhat confident. Usually the higher the confidence levels of the athlete, the better chance of a good performance. Confidence helps, but it does not guarantee good results.

Likewise, some players have an optimistic outlook and others are pessimistic. Optimistic players would say, "My fault, but I'll get them next time," while pessimistic players would say things like, "I'm no good" or "the umpire screwed me." Optimistic people own up to mistakes, while pessimistic people make excuses. I was an example of a player who played and succeeded without much confidence, yet always had an optimistic feeling about where I was headed in my career. Players can succeed and progress without high levels of confidence, but I have never known a successful player who did not have an optimistic outlook.

It would be ideal for coaches to have all players that are confident and optimistic. Rarely, if ever, is this the case. Most players sit in between, where their most recent performance determines how confident they are. Good coaches will help players gain and maintain confidence as often as possible. Most importantly, though, is helping our young develop optimistic outlooks toward their future. As mentioned, sports performance involves much failure, frustration, and losing. Parents and coaches are vital for helping kids remain optimistic in their outlook toward themselves and their future. Players, who remain optimistic and show confidence, play with the poise needed to keep advancing and reach their full potential.

Calming the Storm

Often, parents would cite their player's apparent nervousness as a concern, believing their kid could not perform well because it was in their head. Stated in another way, parents would say, "She/he can do it in practice but not in the game." These are legitimate problems and ones that require time and patience by all to overcome. The good news is that players can get over their nervousness to the point where it does not hinder their play. The first action is to explain to young players that nervous feelings are natural and good. When they feel nervous, it means the adrenaline is flowing. Adrenaline is what gives us a heightened sense of awareness and the energy to perform at a higher level. Additionally, inform players that nervousness is a sign they care and caring is good because they will do something about it if things do not go their way. If they did not care, they would not be nervous. Explain to them that all good players have nervous feelings, so they are not alone.

Good coaches do not recommend that players try to get rid of the nerves, but they try to give players an understanding of the things they can control. It is common for athletes to have a fear of failure, but coaches can explain that players can only control their effort and concentration levels. Complete concentration on an object or task can get their mind off their nervousness and allow them to perform. With the adrenaline already present and the concentration on the ball, they would be able to perform to the best of their ability.

Extreme nervousness usually occurs because of a player's total lack of confidence. Another helpful action is to impress upon them the need to practice their skills more and especially under game-like situations. The more a player has the feeling that they have been there and done that, the less chance their nervousness would get the best of them. I would explain to them that poise can be developed and they could turn their nervousness into poise, over time. Poise is the trait of feeling very comfortable in the situation they are in. Poise does not mean that the person is not nervous, rather they feel like they can handle the stressful situation. As mentioned, all athletes have a fear of failure, but players with poise overcome this fear with a strong desire to perform at their best. Greater confidence neutralizes nerves and this confidence is usually only gained through more practice, which produces success.

Making a Difference

At one time or another, all athletes need reassurance to get through the times when their nerves or lack of confidence get the best of them. As a coach, I was continually saying confidence and optimism-building words to players so they felt better about themselves and they could overcome their uptight feelings. With parent's and coach's help, the development of poise in every athlete is possible.

A few of my favorite sayings I would relate to players would give this reassurance and maintain the player's optimistic outlook.

- Don't worry about the results and stay focused on the task.
- "Remember the good and forget the bad or this game will kill you." (Kill just a figure of speech of course.)
- "You can do it (and do not let anyone tell you that you can't)."
- You are one play away from putting it all together."
- "'How you do' and 'who you are', are two different things."
- "You may have failed the previous time, but it does not mean you will the next time."
- "No excuses"—accept responsibility for your play.
- "No regrets"—work as hard as you can so you do not look back with regret.
- "Look at the bright side, it could have been worse."
- "I want you to imagine how good you will feel when you are able to perform up to your ability level despite the nervousness you feel. That is a great accomplishment itself."
- "I believe in you."

Kids develop self-esteem by hearing positive words from others. Parents and coaches, who say the right things at the right times, will mold their players' attitude in sports and life. The following are other optimistic words and phrases that coaches can use to reduce stress, build poise, and teach life lessons without alienating players.

- "We" is a much less intimidating word than "you." "You have to do this," "You have to practice," or "You will never be any good doing that," are examples of intimidating statements. It is much better to say "We will figure it out," or "We will work on it." Developing the correct skills and knowledge of the game can be very imposing for a young player, and it does not help when singled out. Knowing it is a group project will put less pressure on them and allow them to look forward to continue figuring it out with another in their corner.

✧ "You"—wait a minute, you just said . . . I know but the word you is actually a very persuasive word when used in a positive manner. "You" used in an inspiring way like "You can do it," or "You are the best," is very uplifting to the player.

✧ "Try"—suggesting something with this word is so much better than saying, "do" this. So much of skill development comes with trial and error and using the word try states this. It is difficult for players to want to change something that feels comfortable but by using this word, they are usually more willing to listen to suggestions.

✧ "Remember (the good)"—a great way to put positive feedback into a player's head is to have them recall the good times. Remember that game where you . . . Selective positive memory for an athlete is a good thing and helps them bring back a positive outlook. This is necessary to overcome tough times.

✧ "Forget (the bad)"—once again, selective memory is essential. Great players want to "be there" with the game on the line and a chance to come through, no matter how many times they may have failed in the past. The phrase, "Forget about it," after a bad result is actually an affirming one for players to hear.

✧ "Be yourself"—many parents and coaches want their players to be as they were. It is important adults understand that all players have different personalities. It is one thing to expect players to play with more intensity but another to expect them to be someone they are not.

✧ "Always believe in yourself and do not give up"—there will be times in sports where no one believes the player will come through, but it is important they believe in themselves. I would tell kids that it does not matter if your previous fifteen tries were unsuccessful—you can come through the next time if you believe in yourself.

✧ "Trust" (do not think)—sports require players to react and they must learn to trust their hard work and their natural skills will take over in the heat of the game. Thinking about what one has to do instead of "doing it" will inhibit good reactions. Instincts will come when a player learns to react without having to think. This development of instincts comes quicker for some than others, but all players are capable of developing instincts and trusting their skills. With practice and over time, players will learn to react without thinking.

✧ "See"—this word allows players to focus on the object without thinking about the process. Vision is what allows us to "do" and to focus. Observing an object or action with total concentration will allow the player to focus on the "here and now" and not the "what if."

✧ "Improve, don't prove"—trying to prove a point in the short term and using that as a motivator is ok, but always working to improve will serve one better in the long run.

✧ "Hang in there" or "get them next time"—portraying the never give up and things will get better attitude with these words are valuable encouragement.

Easy, Natural Pep Talks

Not only are these uplifting words for coaches to use with players, but once coaches make them a part of their coaching vocabulary, it becomes very easy for coaches to turn them into inspirational pep talks. The following is an example of an ad-lib pep talk using the positive phrases.

"Guys/Girls, remember, you are not alone. We are a team that wins and loses together. Today, we are going to choose to win. Keep your focus on each play and never give up. If you make a mistake, forget about it and get them the next time. Trust your instincts and skills, believe in yourselves and see clearly the tasks without fear. You have nothing to prove, but work hard to improve and that is all I can ask of you. Give 100% so we will have no regrets and no excuses when the game is over. Hang in there when the going gets tough. You can do this. I believe in you."

The Short and Sweet Motivators

The following words and gestures also build confidence and relieve stress. They need little explanation.

✧ "Yes"
✧ "Sweet" (Good)
✧ "Way to battle"
✧ "Great effort" (Nice try)
✧ "Awesome"
✧ "Nice"

- ✧ "Not bad"
- ✧ "Better"
- ✧ "I'm proud of you"
- ✧ "Wow" (Did you see that?)
- ✧ "Relax" (Clear your mind)
- ✧ High five (Fist pump)
- ✧ Thumbs up
- ✧ The point (One or two fingers at player)
- ✧ A smile (used with all of the above)

Lighten Up the Situation—Using Humor to Relieve Stress

You may have heard the story about a former teammate of mine and great major league pitcher, Rick Sutcliffe, and how he was getting "lit up" pitching one day. After the home team hit a home run, it was customary for fireworks to be set off in celebration. Rick, a member of the visiting team, gave up a couple homeruns, after which pitching coach, Billy Connors, walked out to talk to him. Rick was obviously not in a very good mood, and barked to the coach, "What are you doing out here?" Connors paused and then said, "The manager told me to come out here to give the fireworks people time to reload."

There are times when the best medicine is laughter in order to defuse players' tension. Good coaches recognize when players are giving their all, and they just need time to relax and start over again. Using humor can work well with individuals and teams, letting them know it is just a game and everything will be all right.

The Deflators

The opposite of the positive and optimistic words that people use, of course, are the negative and pessimistic sayings. These phrases tear down confidence and create discouragement and pessimism. They only serve to put a player in a negative frame of mind and are usually accompanied with a demeaning voice. In addition, parents and coaches should avoid using them because they will alienate players from the sport.

- ❖ "What did I just tell you?"—This statement makes a young player feel like a loser. Muscle memory and sporting instincts take a great amount of time to develop and saying something repeatedly will not change their muscle memory. Only practice and experience will change things. Instead coaches should say, "Hang in there," "We will work on it," or "Try it this way."

- ❖ "Why did you do that?"—This may be an ok question to a player later in a one-on-one situation, but only puts a player on the spot in front of everyone. It is much better to say, "Forget about it," or "Get 'em next time."

- ❖ "What were you thinking?"—Most of the time, players will know when they make mistakes, so saying this is unnecessary. Additionally, whether they were thinking or not, it is too late to change their actions now. This statement puts a player in a tough spot with no answer. That is why teams have a coach, to instruct in a positive way when players make mistakes and not ridicule them.

- ❖ "When I was your age, we used to"—This is a favorite of parents and coaches and if their intention is to get kids to roll their eyes, shake their heads and think "here we go again," then use this one. The realization by parents that times have changed and kids are different today is important. For example, kids do not go to the park every-day and play all day like their parents used to. Parents and coaches should not blame kids for the changing times, but can still encourage them to practice and play as much as possible.

✧ "Look at me when I say something"—The assumption, that just because players are not looking at the coach when they are talking means they are not listening, is not always correct. Often, the players who are listening are the ones who are not staring right at them. Some people comprehend things better when they are not looking at the talking person. Asking questions after talking is a good way for the coach to find out who is listening. Questioning players after coaching keeps the pressure on players to pay attention. Keeping instructional talks to a short time span is a good idea with young players. However, it is good advice to encourage kids to make eye contact, especially when the coach is talking directly to them. This eye contact is a sign of respect to the coach and keeps the player on the coach's good side.

✧ "We are going to run when this is over"—There may be a point to be made if there is an apparent lack of hustle but if it is a lack of execution, or winning, it is best to use the time to work on the fundamentals of the game. Nothing will turn a player off to the sport more than too many penalties and unnecessary over-exertions. Running is for conditioning purposes and not penalizing the team.

✧ "You have to"—No one likes to have to do something that another thinks they should do, when put in those terms. It would be much better to make suggestions in a positive manner with the words "we" and "try."

✧ "I can't believe you are so and so's kid"—very unfair statement that speaks for itself. Just because a player's mom or dad were good at something does not mean their child is automatically good or they have the same interests.

✧ "Get your head out of your ___"—unnecessary remark that has no place in youth sports. Coach needs to learn to smile.

Short and Not-So-Sweet

Other negative words and actions that positive coaches avoid: (Remember, body language hurts as much as words.)

✧ The look-away
✧ Head shake
✧ Eye roll
✧ Slamming down or kicking an object
✧ "Come on."
✧ Ignoring players
✧ Palms up with a quizzical look on the face
✧ "That's terrible."

False praise—There is a fine line between positive and false praise. It is positive to recognize effort but false to build up player's performance results with excessive praise when their play was average or below average. Players will recognize the unsubstantiated praise and may lose a little respect for the giver.

Making excuses—parents and coaches should not make excuses and blame outside sources for losing unless they want the players to do the same and develop the same attitude.

Demoralizing Pep Talk

"Guys/Girls, you are embarrassing me. I cannot believe you can play this badly. You have to start doing what I say or we are going to run when this is over. What in the world are you thinking out there? When I was your age I" . . . etc.

I am sure you get the idea. Using some of these negative phrases in your pep talk will turn kids off quickly. Rarely will uninspiring and negative talk cause kids to compete with pride, even if it intimidates them into playing harder. Eventually most kids upon hearing such negative talk, will lose self-esteem and /or their desire to continue playing the sport much longer.

Of Course, It's How You Say It

Many words have positive or negative connotations, depending on the voice spoken in and the words accompanying them. As mentioned earlier about the word "you," the context the word is used in will determine if it is positive or negative. Other examples of words like this are listed below.

- ✧ "Concentrate"—Concentration is obviously important, but the word has little meaning to young players during the game. The word itself takes so much "concentration" to figure out its meaning that the game will probably be over before they figure it out. It would be better to say, "See the ball" or "Relax and react." However, telling the players to concentrate on the task before a game is common and ok.

- ✧ "Think" (while pointing to the head)—this is similar to the previous word. When said during the game and in a negative tone after a player has messed up a play, has a negative connotation to the player. Using it before the game is ok and acceptable. For example, "Use your heads out there." (Think)

✧ "Embarrassing"—I do not recommend the coach or parent saying, "You are embarrassing me," because it puts the attention on them and not the player. It implies that the players are playing only for their coach or parents. Players should be playing to have fun, for each other (teammates), and to win and adults should expect only that. However, saying your "effort level is embarrassing" to older players (ages thirteen and up) is acceptable because it describes something they can control (effort) and not the players themselves.

✧ "Today"—it is very important to keep players in the "here and now" and not on the past or future. This word has a positive and negative connotation. Using it in a positive way like, "Today is a new day, and we cannot do anything about the last game," is good. Saying, "Today," as in "hurry up" is unnecessary.

Always Look at the Bright Side—A Short Story

A father and his boy came to my Academy one day. The dad said to his boy "Brad, how would you like to take some hitting lessons?" Brad replied, "No thanks, dad, they won't be needed because I am going to be the greatest hitter that ever lived." Brad's dad rolled his eyes to which his son said, "Watch, I'll show you." Brad picked up a ball and a bat and proceeded to flip the ball into the air, swung and missed. "That's only strike one," he said. The boy picked up the ball again, flipped it up into the air, swung and missed again. "Only strike two," he said. This time he picked up the ball, hesitated and really concentrated on it before he flipped it up once again. Brad swung as hard as he could and fell down after missing it, for the third strike. Now everyone around felt a little sorry for the boy, especially dad. The boy looked up and said, "I may not be the greatest hitter that ever lived . . . but I am going to be the greatest pitcher, because I just struck out one heck of a hitter."

—Author Unknown

We all should have such an optimistic outlook when things do not go as planned.

9

Team—"That's What We Do, We Pick Each Other Up"

Unforgettable Teammate

One of my favorite teammates was a player whom I never knew very well. I joined the Triple A baseball team mid-season and was with a new baseball organization. Joe De Sa really had no reason to stick up for me. Here is what happened. One night, when turning a double play, the runner for the opposing team cross-body blocked me, hitting my planted front leg. It was an obvious illegal slide and one that put me on the disabled list for quite some time. The following evening, Joe De Sa came up to bat in the first inning. Joe was a power-hitting first baseman who hit homeruns and drove in runs. With nobody on base Joe unexpectedly squared around to bunt. He bunted the ball to the first baseman who easily picked the ball up and flipped the ball to the second baseman. The second baseman, covering the bag, happened to be the abusive runner from the previous night, which of course Joe

There is no "I" in team

knew. Upon arriving at first base, Joe "accidentally" raised his forearm to the second baseman's chest. This blow knocked the second baseman down and caused both benches to clear. Being on crutches and unable to attend the game, I was told of Joe's action after the game by other teammates. It almost brought a tear to my eye that a teammate whom I hardly knew would stand up for the team and me like that. Joe taught us all the meaning of team and team pride that night.

Although I do not recommend retaliation and unsportsmanlike play in amateur baseball, it is sometimes necessary at the highest levels of sport. The story has a sad ending though, as later that year, Joe De Sa was tragically killed in a car accident. I will never forget Joe.

All for One and One for All

ONE OF THE FIRST THINGS a player learns when he gets to the big leagues is about the importance of the team. Even if a player has a good day individually and the team loses, a player should not act happy and self-satisfied. And vice versa, they should not act down after having a rough game personally, if the team won. It is a business at this level where winning is what it is all about. You would think players at the highest level would have already learned this, but it is not that simple. In order to get to that level of play, players had to focus so much on their own performance over the years, and even though they are playing team sports, individual performance is still necessary to continue moving up the sports ladder and to get to the top.

One of the coach's greatest challenges is to integrate the individual goals into the team concept. This is a tougher thing for professional coaches to deal with then one would think. In order to stay at the top-level, players have to continue to produce.

Additionally, it is human nature for individuals to want to perform well and feel good about it when they do. Add in the fact that so much money and adulation is involved and you begin to recognize some of the distractions involved for the pro players. Multiply these issues by the number of players on the team and you see what a challenge professional coaches face in order to corral everyone into a team. Coaches certainly want each player to perform well and are happy for them when they do, but they also want to promote the feeling to the players collectively, that team and winning are what is important and that it is not all about personal accomplishment.

Fortunately, coaches of amateur teams and young players do not have to deal with the money and fame, at least not at the levels of the professional game. Molding individuals into a team is still a formidable task for the coach. Most amateur coaches realize winning is not everything, yet it is the reward for performing better than the opposition and a sign of a well-prepared (coached) team. When there has to be a winner and a loser, teams and individuals should have the integrity to do their best to win and that is what the coach tries to get across to the players.

You will often read about teams that have good chemistry. This means that most, if not all, of the individuals on the team focus on winning and being there for each other. They want to do well individually, but they are more concerned with winning and team goals than individual achievements. It takes a very good manager and organization to get everybody on the same page. The best coaches often do it, but it also takes the cooperation of very mature and dedicated players. From experience, I know there is no better feeling in sports than to win a championship and teams win championships with all players contributing and pulling for one another. That is why you see heartfelt elation when a team wins a championship.

Together, Anything is Possible

Players at a young age should be happy when they perform well, but it is also important for parents and coaches to nurture the idea that the players are part of something bigger than they are individually. The concept of team and teamwork will serve kids in many phases of their lives and in many areas of eventual work and career. Whether it is team or individual sports, many people are involved in the player's career. Sports can provide players the understanding that working together is important, and that it often takes the contributions of many to get the job done. One of the essential goals of coaches is imparting the understanding to team members that working with others to accomplish a goal is a worthy and great pursuit.

Another great thing about sports is the opportunity to build relationships along the way. Often, when a player hangs up the spikes, they state that what they will miss the most is just being around their teammates. This is the same feeling that most kids experience while playing on a team. The best part is the hanging out with teammates and friends, having fun and being part of something—a team. All kids want the opportunity to play, but just as important for most is the social interaction that sports provide.

Most young athletes will not play into high school and fewer beyond, but the lessons of teamwork and social interaction are vital in their development and eventual pursuits. Additionally, the friendships made playing sports will form bonds that last a long time and maybe even a lifetime.

Promoting the Team Concept:

The following are things coaches and parents can do to help instill the importance of team in players' minds:

- Say, "That's nice you won," or "Tough loss," as one of the first things to your son or daughter after the game. This promotes the idea that the group (team) is important. In contrast, parents often ask, "How did you do?" as the first thing after a game.

- Likewise, conversations with your son or daughter should include talk about the team as a whole and not just their individual performance. Questions like "How did the team feel after the game?" or "What does the team need to do to improve?" are good examples.

- Mention an unselfish play by a player that helped the team or recognize a player battling through a minor injury in order to continue helping the team.

- Encourage your son or daughter to congratulate all members of the team in good times, and pat teammates on the back during rough times.

- Have team "get togethers" as often as possible, and encourage all team members to attend. (Go to movies, the pool, or similar activities together.)

- Explain to the players that not every one can be a star player, but that everyone is important to the team's success and to the star's success.

- Encourage players to get to know all team members. Adults should watch for and discourage cliques on the team. (Cliques are small groups that tend to only associate with each other by excluding others.)

- Watch for players who are loners and try to get others to include them.

- Match up players of different ability levels together as partners when practicing and when having contests among the team.

- Encourage players to recognize other team members' contributions when talking to friends or during interviews with the media, as well as being gracious toward the opponent.

Creating a Season to Remember:

The following are other options that coaches can consider in order to create team cohesiveness and fun. Team social interaction helps build solidarity and connections that help players bond as friends and teammates.

- Set up a fantasy league for your team using professional players. Keep it simple. League lasts until the young player league is over.

- Instead of canceling practice on a rainy day, meet at the house and have a video game contest.

- At the first practice each week, have players pick a professional team they think will not lose—winner is player whose team goes the longest from that day without losing.

- Early in the season, have the team come up with the team's signature congratulatory gesture (high five, fist pump, or something original), that is exclusive to the team.

- Take team to a local high school or college game. Encourage the players to cheer so they stay attentive to the game. Pointing out the techniques of the players by the kid's coach is good. After watching awhile, the team has their regular practice.

✧ Coach hands out a professional sport's card at the end of each "practice" (not game) to the player with the best offensive play, defensive play, and best hustle for that day.

✧ Set up a parent–son or daughter game. Keep it safe. (This also serves to remind parents that the game is not as easy as it looks.)

✧ Have a players autograph day. Coach hands out pictures (of players in uniform) to all family members of players, and coach picks a day where players will sign their autograph before the selected game.

✧ Have a few parents with video cameras film an intra-squad game, film player introductions, and pre and post-game interviews. Close-up shots of players when possible. Next rainy day watch it with players.

✧ Let the players design a practice. They can choose what to work on and for how long. No regular game allowed.

✧ Along the same lines, have the players do some of the coaching. Ask players to volunteer to give short talks on an aspect of the particular sport. (One of my greatest joys at summer camps was seeing young players interact as they coached themselves in ball games where they had no adult coach involved.)

✧ Home run trot contest, best end-zone celebration, or sport specific demonstration. Each player has a shot at giving his best demonstration. Players are the judges.

✧ Have a picture day. Have players bring in a picture of whatever sport related topic the coach picks.

✧ Stump the coaches. Players try to stump the coaches with sport-specific trivia questions. Each player gets one question. Number of misses by coach determines how many laps the coaches have to run.

✧ Have a charity day for the team where the team does something nice for an individual or organization.

It's Not That You Fall, It's Getting Up That Counts— Overcoming Adversity

Most people who follow sports know Florida Marlins All Star second baseman, Dan Uggla, had a rough 2008 All Star game, which is evidence that poor performances happen to even the best players. What most people do not know are his quotes after that game. When asked what his teammates said to him after the game he remarked, "A lot of guys come up and slap you on the leg and pick you up, that's what we do. We pick each other up."

We pick each other up. That is what we do. What a great explanation of what it means to be a team and how the lessons that sports teach will influence how our young athletes live. Good parents and coaches help players through adverse times and they should encourage their players to pick up their teammates too. Coaches and parents can certainly help players at these times, but help from teammates at these moments is probably the most helpful thing to a struggling player's mental state. Each time an athlete overcomes adversity, it will usually make them mentally stronger for the next time adversity comes. This stronger player will now have the experience to pass on to others who struggle in the future. Picking up a teammate is often a learned skill, and then passed on.

I had a teammate who needed to be picked up. You will understand after reading the story below. As mentioned, that is what we do, and we write about it, and never let them forget about it.

The following is a true story from the Murray State University student newspaper which appeared March 21, 1974, written by another teammate of ours, John Erardi. John is currently a great writer for the *Cincinnati Enquirer*. You will see why.

He is Legend

Bobby Mantooth plays centerfield for the Murray State University Breds baseball team. On Monday, in the first game of a doubleheader against the University of Chicago, he did something I never saw done before—and I don't suspect I'll ever see again.

With his team at bat in the bottom of the third inning, "Tooth," as his teammates call him, did the unheard of. He made all three outs.

Now, for those who don't understand the finer points of our National Pastime, let me explain. Everybody had heard the saying, "Three strikes and you're out." Well, after three outs the inning is over, and the team batting is out.

Normally, in a given inning, three different hitters each make a separate out, and the inning is over. Occasionally, but extremely rarely, you might see one guy account for two outs. Never before had I seen one player make all three outs.

That was before the immortal "Tooth" came along. Now I've seen everything.

Blastin' Bobby is a cool dude. He is class personified. "Major League" emanates from every pore in his body. His mustache is Big League, his hairstyle is Big League, his stance at the plate is Big League.

He's the kind of guy baseball fanatics name their kids after. He's the hero of sports novels. Young boys trade away five or six bubble-gum cards just to get one of the "Tooth."

The name of his game is "fluidity." His claim to fame is a picture-perfect swing that cuts the air like a machete whistling away under-brush in the jungle. He is smooth with a capital "S."

For all the this, "Tooth" is not the kind of ballplayer one would expect to find under the category of "Most Outs Made in One Inning by a Breds Batsman." Great ballplayers set great records. Unfortunately, this wasn't the movies.

I've got to admit, though, such is the stuff movies are made of. The bottom of the third inning had "Tooth" written all over it.

The first time up, he ripped a screaming rope right at the Chicago shortstop, one out.

The next eight Breds reached base safely.

Bobby M. stepped up again. Before entering the batter's box, he performed what has come to be called the "Mantooth Stretch," a curious looking back-and-forth rotation of the neck as if he were a cobra preparing to strike.

He lashed a shot deep to right center, only to be robbed again of a base hit by another fielder. Two outs.

Returning to the dugout, "Tooth" was the target of some good natured ribbing from his teammates. There were a few cracks about his chances of getting another time at bat. Nobody really thought he would.

Once again, however, the next eight Breds reached base safely. It looked like a merry-go-round in the infield. A whopping 14 runs had crossed the plate. MSU led 19–1.

Amidst catcalls from his teammates, and a big collective sigh of relief from the Chicago ballclub, "Tooth" strode to the plate, wearing a grin as wide as the margin on the scoreboard. He had no intention whatsoever of making the third out.

The first pitch was a curve outside. Ball one. Next came a fastball up and in. Ball two.

"Tooth" ripped at the third pitch with his trademark swing, but missed.

Another ball, then a called strike two. The count had run to three balls and two strikes, a full count. You could have heard a gum bubble pop in the Murray dugout. It was as if the score was tied and this was the final inning of the World Series. Only everybody was rooting against the "Tooth" getting a hit.

He didn't let anybody down. The historic pitch was about chin high, just out of the strike zone. "Tooth" known for a keen eye, saw before the pitch reached the plate that a split second decision would determine his fate. This was no time for soliloquies. Either he would be a goat and take a free pass to first base or a hero by taking a gamble and swinging.

Bobby is a gambler. He put his 34 inch Louisville Slugger into motion with the whip-like quickness only he could author. An audible groan could be heard as he swung right through the ball.

Just like Casey in *Casey at the Bat,* Mighty Mantooth had struck out. But unlike Casey, for whom, "there was no joy in Mudville" as the poem goes, Bobby may ride his classic feat all the way to the Baseball Hall of Shame in Bummersville, N.Y.

As Mantooth's agent, I just got a letter from the Commissioner of Baseball, Bowie Kuhn, which says "Tooth" has been assured of a niche in the hall right next to the only other MSU athlete to earn the honor.

How many of you out there remember Fitzhugh "Iron Gut" McGillicutty, a pitcher for the Breds back at the turn of the century?

In 1901, "Iron Gut" once ate 8,000 Twinkies in between losing both games of a doubleheader by identical scores of 42–1. Both the Twinkies and the 84 runs scored in one day are still MSU records.

— John Erardi

Bobby Mantooth has gone on to become a great coach in the state of Kentucky.

The Times Are a Traveling

Homesick Blues

HAVING NEVER BEEN OUT OF THE COUNTRY, I was quite excited when I had the opportunity to play winter baseball in Mexico in 1980. I arrived late one evening at the Mexican airport, where I was supposed to be picked up by a team representative for the two-hour car ride to the town I was to play in. I waited and waited for the ride that never came. Only able to speak a little German, the foreign language I took in high school and English of course, I was feeling helpless and a little nervous. Fortunately, I recognized another ball player from the United States and he let me tag along with him for the night as he was playing in the local town. I am not sure what I would have done without him. The worst part of the trip, however, was yet to come.

The following day, I was eventually picked up and driven to my team's city. Upon arriving, I was told the bus was leaving in an hour for a little goodwill game the team had scheduled. The bus

A Traveling Nightmare

trip out of town was interesting, as there were many stops to pick up some of our ballplayers as we passed through town. A couple hours outside of town, we stopped in an open field where there appeared to be a town picnic. Ok. No baseball field, no backstop, no dugouts, no fence for fan protection, no problem—just throw down a couple makeshift bases and let the game begin. This was not the typical picture of pro baseball, but it was baseball I remembered playing as a kid. That no one (fans, coaches, players) was injured was truly remarkable. The temperature was one hundred degrees outside and knowing not to drink the water, I proceeded to drink about five sodas that day. I did not feel very good on the bus trip back. Even this was not the worst part of the trip.

Upon arriving back at our hotel, I met my new roommate, "Super Joe" Charbonneau. Yes, *the* "Super Joe," famous for opening glass bottles with his eye socket, chewing glass, and fighting bums in railroad cars when growing up, and the "Joe" who would become the 1980 American League Rookie of the Year. They say opposites attract and that was the case as Joe and I hit it off and became good friends. The worst part of my travel ball experience happened a few days later when I ended up in the hospital for a week. After a ball game one night, I decided to fry up the fish I had proudly caught in the Pacific Ocean. After warming up the oil and taking a shower, I returned to the kitchen to find the cabinets lit up. Mindlessly, I struck the pan to douse the fire only to have the grease fly all over my unclothed body. Obviously, being far away from home and all my loved ones was not a joyous time. I did make the local newspapers though with the headline "Perconte, look out for the fish." I felt very far from home for a while, but things settled as the fans, teammates, and town people made me feel at home quickly.

Most people think of professional sports as a glamorous life. It is for the most part, especially for the players at the highest levels. I was often asked during my playing days what the best and worst part of pro baseball was. My answer was the same for both questions—the travel. The great cities and countries the game took me to were exciting. However, the hassles and constant travel, along with being away from family, diminished the excitement of it. At the minor league level of professional sports, though, the life can be far from glamorous. Most players at the lower levels can tell you about the all-night bus trips and early morning flights arriving just in time to put on the uniform and play. The best part about travel in the minor leagues is the stories it produces for years to come, like the one on the previous page.

Road Warriors

The farthest I ever remember traveling for a sporting event as a kid was about twenty miles and that was to a regional tournament. Years ago, unless a player was on a very good team where their team kept advancing in the one tournament a year, the chance of traveling very far for a sporting event was remote. Jump ahead quite a few years. It is common for young players of today to get around, so to speak. I know my kids' teams had been to Florida, South Carolina, Wisconsin, Michigan, Colorado, Florida, Kentucky, Ohio, Iowa, Missouri, and Indiana before the age of seventeen because of sporting tournaments.

Probably the biggest change in youth sports over the past twenty years has been the great number of select traveling sports teams that are available for players of all ages. Years ago, the only option for players was to play in their local in-house recreational leagues and schools. The local leagues are still available for players today, but there now exists the opportunity to play for select travel teams. This travel phenomenon has created tough decisions for parents and players. Decisions about whether to play travel, what age to begin, what is too much, among others, present a challenge for families. Making the wrong decision can lead to upsetting results for young players. The wrong decision may cause an unhappy player, family fighting, or even the end of the player's desire to continue playing that sport altogether. Many players have benefited and had good experiences playing travel, but many have dreaded the experience too.

Travel ball has become popular for a number of reasons. Mainly, a need for travel arose because of some imagined or real deficiencies of the in-house leagues. Many in-house leagues and sports failed to keep up with the demands of the players and parents over the necessity for more games and better competition. For the most part, travel ball has led to a greater number of kids that have been able to participate and has given the upper tier of players a better opportunity to improve their skills. People who think travel ball would eliminate all the things they did not like about the regular in-house league may be disappointed. It is wise for them to be prepared for some possible negative experiences along the way. There are many horror stories in travel ball about overzealous coaches and parents. Of course, there are overzealous people in the in-house recreational leagues, also, but the occurrence is more prevalent in the travel leagues because of the greater commitment that is often involved in travel ball.

Speed Bumps

I have experienced travel ball as both a parent and a coach. Keeping everyone happy from players to parents to other coaches can be very challenging. Of course, that is no different from the regular in-house leagues either. The difference comes about because people tend to expect a professional atmosphere just because the word travel is associated with the team, league, or tournament. The difference is the expectations are often unrealistic at the select travel level. In addition, people have a tendency to expect the coach or coaches to have more experience and knowledge because it is travel ball. People interested in travel ball should understand that coaches might be no more qualified than any other parent is, and are only coaching travel because of their disenchantment with the recreational league. Some coaches start a travel team for their own child's benefit. This way they can play their son or daughter where and when they want. Other travel coaches believe travel is all about winning and believe that if winning is "not the most important thing" for the player and player's parents, they should not be in the travel program. Such a coach's number one concern is winning at the expense of player development and fun. Another interesting aspect of the travel phenomenon is that people expect every player to be travel caliber and believe it is ok to show disgust over a player's play because it is "travel ball." In addition, expectations tend to be higher for travel because of the higher fees involved. Because of this fee, many parents believe they have the right to express their feelings whenever they want. It is important for parents and players on travel teams to keep everything in perspective and that having fun, developing skills and just having the chance to compete are what is important.

Good Travel, Bad Travel

Often, the advantages of playing travel for some turn out to be disadvantages for others. For instance:

More games and practices:

Advantage—Players improve skills and increase game knowledge.

Disadvantage—physically and emotionally tired players may become burned out.

Better players and better competition:

Advantage—Quicker improvement for some players.

Disadvantage—Discouragement for those unable to keep up with the skill levels necessary to remain successful. Those unable to keep up may have remained a star in the regular league where their enjoyment and willingness to keep playing will have lasted much longer.

More tournaments and big games of travel:

Advantage—Players are often more prepared and pressure ready, which may make them more prepared for the pressures of high school and college competition.

Disadvantage—overwhelming for players, especially those who do not handle pressure very well.

Choosing the Coach:

Advantage—there is a greater possibility of getting the coach the player wants in travel ball because of the ability to try out for the team the coach is coaching. As mentioned, a good coach makes the season more beneficial to a player's development, interest, and future in a sport.

Disadvantage—Having games and practices with coaches who are negative is hardly bearable for the shorter in-house season and is entirely unbearable for the longer and more intense travel season.

Weighing All Options

One of the most frequently asked questions I would receive from my students' parents was:

Should we be playing travel? It was appropriate that they said "we" because travel ball requires a commitment from other family members too, not just the player. My initial response was, "Is this their favorite sport?" As long as it was their favorite, I encouraged them to consider it if they knew of a good coach or program, and if their child was travel caliber. I would especially recommend it for the families of female athletes. There is a much bigger skill level gap for girls entering high school between those that have played travel as opposed to those who have only played the in-house, recreational league. For the male athlete, the skill gap is not as prominent, so the necessity of playing travel is not as clear-cut.

There are many decisions to make for families considering playing travel. Below are the most common questions and some suggestions to help answer those questions. (Obviously, some of these questions apply to the regular in-house leagues also. They tend to be greater issues in travel ball though, because of the greater commitment involved.)

Is travel ball for your son or daughter? The over-riding reason for playing on a select travel team should be the child's interest in playing. This may seem obvious, but often it is the parent's interest in their child playing and not the kid's. Determining a kid's interest and why is the first thing to do. When a player displays interest in playing travel ball, the reason should be along the lines of really enjoying or loving to play that sport. Often, when this is not the reason, a player will get into the travel season and show disinterest because it was not their decision to play, but their parent's, or it was not the sport they enjoyed the most. In either case, boredom sets in and the season gets very long, quickly. Playing travel ball before a player wants to commit extra time to that sport can be counter-productive. Many players grow into a love of a sport and it is at that time they should begin travel ball.

Additionally, it is not a good reason to play just because the child's friends are playing or because a good friend's mom or dad is coaching. Generally, children who want to play only to have fun and be around their friends should not be playing travel. Recreational leagues are for those children. Fun and friends are important at all levels of youth sports, but there should be a higher commitment for playing travel ball.

It is equally important that parents do not put their child in a level of ball that they are not ready for talent-wise. Players who are in over their head will face much discouragement. Players should at least be in the upper half, ability-wise, for their age group. Parents tend to overestimate their child's skill level so an outside opinion may be necessary to make this determination. It does not hurt to have players try out for travel teams, but all should be prepared for the rejection that may come if they do not make the team.

Also, just because a player is one of the best players does not mean the player must play travel ball. It is ok to remain a big fish (a star) in the smaller pond (in-house league) if they are not totally devoted or interested in the added commitment of travel ball. On the other hand, the player who totally dominates the in-house league, and does not seem challenged, probably should be playing travel ball. Otherwise, they may become bored with being too good, if that is possible. I have run into parents who are very proud that their child has an .850 batting average and they should be proud. Their child is probably ready for an increased challenge, though.

What is a good age to begin? This can be a difficult call because there is no set age that is best for playing travel ball. The main concern should be the number of games the team plans on playing and the philosophies of the coaches. Overdoing it at a young age with too many games and tournaments can make young players physically and emotionally drained. This could turn some players off toward their future in the sport. At a young age, the emphasis should be on fun and player development, with smaller emphasis on winning.

Is the quality of ball higher at the travel level than the in-house league? Generally, yes. Travel players are very committed to the sport and are usually hand-picked at tryouts. However, travel teams will often play against teams that are the exact same ages, so it may not be any more challenging than in the recreational league where different age groups are playing. For example, many recreational leagues combine the ten, eleven, and twelve-year-olds together. This can be very challenging for the younger players in the league. The older players have a big advantage in these leagues, so when the player becomes the oldest player in the league that may be a good time to give travel ball a try.

Who are the coaches? Getting your son or daughter the opportunity to play for knowledgeable, dedicated, and fun coaches is the best-case scenario for any athlete and athlete's parents. Having an outstanding coach can make the difference in, not only the child's immediate career, but for their whole life. Great coaches are rare, but there are very good ones in travel ball and in the in-house recreational leagues. For those who do not have the opportunity to play for a great coach, there are a number of factors to consider, understanding the coach can make or break the player's desire and enjoyment of the sport. Getting a bad coach can be just as disastrous for the child's future in that sport, as much as the advantage of having the great coach.

The first thing parents should do is attempt to find out the philosophy of the coaches who will be heading the travel team. When possible, parents can talk to other parents whose child has played for the coach to find out what kind of person and coach they are. Attending a game or two when the coaches are coaching, no matter which sport it is, can accomplish this. The three main objectives of a coaching staff should be player development, winning, and fun. It is important to find out how much emphasis the prospective coach puts on these objectives and how that meshes with you and your child's objectives. I recommend that parents keep in mind not all parents and families have the same philosophy and objectives. Even for parents of the same child, I have seen where a player's mom wants one type of coach and the player's dad wants a coach with a different philosophy. People think everybody wants a coach who puts player development and fun first, but this is not always the case. Some parents believe winning as much as possible is important, and they are not as concerned with equal playing time and fairness for all players. Because of different philosophies, it is important that parents discuss these issues before deciding on a team or coach.

In addition, trying to find the answers to the following questions is helpful for parents in their choice of teams and programs.

Finding these answers will help avoid surprises during the season. Failing to do so can cause uncomfortable situations to occur over the coach's treatment of their child. Once parents find these answers, they can evaluate them and then decide whether the coaches fit you and your child's objectives for playing travel ball.

Other Traveling Issues

Is the coach a win-at-all-cost coach? Coaches who are a win-at-all-cost will only play the best players in the important games and may risk a player's health in the process. Parents should avoid this type of coach unless they have the same philosophy and the team is at the highest level of competition. This type of win-at-all-cost team should only exist at the varsity high school level and older.

Does the coaching staff seem to know the game and spend the time imparting this knowledge to the players? Obviously, coaches who care about players even beyond the playing field are best, but the most important thing is to have knowledgeable coaches who teach the game.

How many players does the team carry and do all the players play an equal amount? Some travel teams carry too many players, while others try to scrape by with the bare minimum. Both scenarios have their obvious faults. The number of players is essential to know for a couple of reasons. For teams with the bare minimum, if your child has to miss a few games or tournaments, the team may be short of players. For teams with an abundance of players, some may not get enough playing time, especially when they are not performing well. In-house leagues have rules that players have to play so much, but that is usually not the case with travel teams. Travel coaches determine how often each player plays. Most kids just want to play, even if their quality of play is not up to standard, and parents want them to play no matter what. Problems usually arise if a player is not getting their fair share of playing time.

Do players get the opportunity to play different positions? At younger ages, it is best if players get an opportunity to play different positions, at least in practice.

How do the coaches react after losing and winning games/tournaments? There is enough pressure on kids during the games that they do not need to go home feeling lousy because of the coach's reactions after the games.

Are the coach's objectives appropriate for the age of the players? As mentioned, there should be a great amount of emphasis on skill development and fun at the pre-high school ages.

Do the players seem to have fun before, during, and after games? All three times are important for maintaining the player's love of the game.

Remember, parents and players can avoid stress and disappointment if they find the answers to these questions before they commit to playing, as opposed to finding out during the season.

Is the whole family committed to the travel idea? Sometimes, sacrifices are necessary by all family members because of the added commitment of time, expense, and pressure involved. Most travel teams play more games, have a longer season and practice over a longer period. It is important that parents do not let the travel team rule their families and adversely affect other kids in the family who are not playing travel ball. Resentment can build up in the non-travel family member(s) when too much attention is given to the travel player's schedule.

Additionally, there is usually a greater expense involved including gas, hotel rooms, and meals, not to mention the cost of playing on the team is usually greater than the local community league. A discussion of these issues of excess time, travel, and expense should take place before committing to playing. For example, figuring out how the player will get to ball games and how they will pay for it are important things to know before signing up. (Many travel teams do a good job of fundraising so the cost remains low. Parents should check into that with each particular team also.)

In-house leagues have a regular season and then playoffs. In travel ball, there are tournaments almost weekly. Families considering travel ball should understand there is usually a higher stress level involved because of the greater number of tournament games. This frequent playoff-type atmosphere is one of the lures of playing travel, but the added stress levels place unwanted tension on some families.

Is travel ball necessary for a player to make the high school team? Rarely will that be a deciding factor. Most high school coaches are unaware and do not care if players have played travel before high school. Most coaches will pick their teams based on what they see at the tryout. Players with the skills and strength to play high school level generally make the team regardless of having played travel or not.

The exception would be the high school where the coaches may be involved in a local travel team. At these schools where coaches also coach off-season travel teams, it usually is an advantage to be playing travel ball. (As mentioned earlier, playing travel for females usually gives them a greater advantage in making the high school team because of the greater skill level of female travel teams compared to the recreational leagues.)

Will playing travel ball make the difference for a player getting a college scholarship? It will not for above-average players. They will get the opportunity whether they play travel or not. They will get to play beyond high school if the desire and grades are there. However, travel ball may give players a few more choices of colleges because of the added exposure.

For the average player, travel ball may give them exposure they may not get in their high school season. Of course, added exposure may hurt some player's chances if they are having trouble competing at the advanced travel level.

As you have noticed, there is much to be considered when deciding whether to play travel ball or not. Every family's situation is different and every kid is different, so each player and their family have to decide what is best for them. Generally, kids can return to the regular in-house leagues if the travel does not work out. Parents should express to their kid that there is no shame in going back to the in-house league after playing travel if they still enjoy playing.

Finally, because of all the excess time and travel that families spend together with other families on the travel team, deeper friendships are often made. A bond is often formed between teammates and teammates' families that last forever. This type of bond says, "We did something special together" and "We will always have those memories to remember and share."

Teaching Moments and Life Lessons

~~~~~~

Pep Talk—Email Style

"I know you are disappointed so far, but remember, that's the best part of sports—they allow us to overcome adversity and meet the challenges along the way—you will appreciate the good times so much more. I know you have worked hard, but it is time to work harder. Then if the results are not good, they will be easier to accept knowing you gave your all. But the results and confidence will probably follow."

"I know you are disappointed. I have been there many times and it is tough. I was the absolute worst player in the league one year and it was a long year. Things change and you have to keep believing in yourself. We always believe in you and are always proud of you. This is a tough test, but you are strong enough to get through it. Keep your head up—it will turn around. You are one of the best clutch players I have ever seen, so when your team needs you most, you will be there for them."

"The game is still testing you—don't let it get the best of you and don't feel like you are letting any one down—your effort is the only thing you can control and that is something that you are great at—believe, me I have played a lot worse then you ever have and played scared. Remember, "No fear." The great pitcher Tom Seaver once said, "Don't ask for an easy life, ask to be strong."

"Don't ever feel like you are letting us down here at home—you always make us proud—the same with your brother and sister—when they hurt, we (Mom and Dad) hurt a little, but we are still so proud of you guys. Keep your head up—smile—believe with no fear—I believe you are going to play as long as you want to play."

THESE ARE SOME OF THE EMAILS sent from a concerned parent to his "down in the dumps" athlete son. The goal was helping his son. Just as important, it served as therapy for the parent who felt the pain of the struggling player. As mentioned previously, when players struggle, their parents feel their mental pain, some more than others do. Parents who want to ease their own feelings and help their player can turn to the internet. Even though we often long for the simpler, pre-computer days, there is nothing better than being able to send an email or text massage to communicate thoughts that would be difficult to say. Parents may not want to send the email too soon after the player struggles, but it is good to write it and review it to be sure it conveys exactly what you want it to say before sending. The act of writing a helpful message, even if you don't send it, can help parents get past their own upset feelings. Most kids do not want to listen to a lecture or pep talk from mom or dad over the phone or in person. However, they will read an email and usually appreciate it when they realize you are just trying to help. Another advantage of the email is there is less risk of saying something that hurts your child or saying something that you will regret having said. Emails can be less intrusive in their kid's life and do not force the kid to have to get into a deep discussion, which most kids do not want to do. The email is something they can refer back to from time to time also. A child does not have to be away for parents to use email to communicate with their kids. Sending encouraging emails and/or text messages to your son or daughter, even when they are at home, can be an effective way of communicating your support, too. Like everything, do not over-do it—too many emails or text messages can become trite, and lose the desired effect.

Listen and Observe

I am sure you have figured out by now that raising an athlete is not easy, especially the athlete who has love for the game. Navigating the bumps and bruises that sports present along the way is challenging for all. What can make parents' decisions even tougher is finding out what their kids' desires truly are. Often, kids may not know what they like and want, and/or have a hard time expressing it. Parents like to think they know what their kids want, yet it is never a sure thing. At times, parents may be surprised to find out that their kids' desires are not what they thought they were. My wife and I were very surprised at our daughter's reaction when she was cut from her high school volleyball team. It was only then that we realized that her favorite sport was volleyball and not softball. The latter sport was the one that we were always focused on, and the one which she was playing much of the year.

Often, I would encounter a parent who would state that their child "eats, sleeps, and drinks the game" only to find a very disinterested player when I practiced with them. Sometimes it is obvious what kids like doing, but other times it is difficult to know, especially as they reach teenage years. Kids will say something because they know that is what mom and dad want to hear. The best indicator of a kid's desire is the player's body language when performing and their excitement level immediately after practice or games. Along with listening to what their kids say, parents should look for these indicators to help them figure out their child's desires. Parents will make mistakes along the way. I know I offered advice that seemed appropriate at the time but, in hindsight, the advice actually made the situation worse. Learning from our mistakes and not repeating them is important for parents too.

Character Building Begins at Home

There is a famous saying from sportswriter Haywood Hale Broun that goes, "Sports do not build character, they reveal it." How true, but the character had to be learned somewhere. A player will reveal the character that they have learned, or failed to learn, from their parents and coaches. This character will present itself on the playing fields. The teachings of the role models (parents and coaches) in players' lives will determine if they learn the life lessons necessary to someday be productive parents themselves. It is important for parents, primarily, to recognize these character-building situations and use their best judgment on how to deal with them. Too often, parents expect their child's coaches and teachers to deal with these teaching moments. I have experienced many situations where parents get irate with the coach for not taking care of an issue, when, it was a parent-teaching moment and not the coach's responsibility. Parents' being there for their sons and daughters at these times is what teaches them about sportsmanship, fairness, leadership, friendship, teamwork, hard work, responsibility, and on and on and is essential to a player's life development. Of course, being there does not mean they have to be physically present at all times; rather they should "be there" with advice and guidance when they hear about situations their kids encounter. This is not to say that coaches should not provide guidance, but it is the parents' job first. Good coaches will reinforce many of these teaching moments and, of course, are responsible for looking for and dealing with any type of bullying, exclusionary, dishonest, or cliquish behavior by the players on the team.

Sportsmanship

Sportsmanship is all about fairness and respect. Often, people assume sportsmanship only applies to sports, but a lack of sportsmanship occurs in many areas of life. People who do not practice respect and fair play in everyday life obviously will not show it on the playing fields. Kids who do not learn to respect others, their opportunities and the game itself, grow into coaches and parents who lack the respect and fairness on the playing field. Teaching fairness and respect in all areas of life is essential. Teaching kids about fairness and respect at home and school is a worthy goal. These teachings of "sportsmanship" will then show up in the child's sports activities. Sportsmanship on the field will be a natural extension of their everyday lives.

It is equally important for parents to display sportsmanship and point out poor displays of it when attending ball games. All too often I have observed people being disrespectful at professional games. For example, one fan begins to yell at the umpire or at an opposing player and everyone around laughs, as if it is funny. Then many of the surrounding fans join in with verbal abuse of the referees or players. Kids in the area often see this behavior and think it is acceptable and a new cycle of disrespectful fans has begun. Parents should not allow kids to think this verbally abusive behavior is funny or acceptable.

Leadership

Hand in hand with sportsmanship, players should be encouraged to become leaders at home, school, and with the team. Not every player can be a star player, but most kids have some leadership skills that they can utilize. Understanding that they do not have to be a star player to be a team leader and they can use the leadership skills they possess are great lessons for kids to learn. Some kids are more vocal and should be encouraged to use their voice in positive ways. Others are quiet but can be encouraged to lead by example and behind the scenes. Others are more social and should be encouraged to organize team functions. Some have a good sense of humor and should be encouraged to keep the team loose. Each player has different gifts and parents and coaches should encourage them to share their gifts with the team. Good coaches will get to know their players' personalities so they can recognize what leadership gifts each player can bring to the team.

Parent Behavior During Games

As mentioned, parents and coaches who show respect for other coaches, players, and umpires are necessary in order to expect players to play with the ideals of sportsmanship.

·(ö)· Things Parents Can Do:

✧ Strive to get their child to games and practices on time.
✧ Let coaches know as soon as possible when a player cannot make a game or practice.

✧ Cheer for own team without going overboard and never root for the other team's players to make mistakes.

✧ Cheer for all players who make a great play or who are injured.

✧ Never yell negative words at the umpire.

✧ Do not argue with other fans.

✧ Do not gloat after a win. Obviously, it is ok to show happiness after a win, without rubbing it in while celebrating.

✧ Words of encouragement are good, but too many, if any, words of how-to instruction during games are not.

✧ Congratulate the winning team and be gracious to the losing team.

✧ Thank all coaches, umpires, and league officials when appropriate.

✧ Handle decisions by coaches, referees, and league officials with class. Discuss all issues with civility.

Being There

This book has already dealt with many teaching moments. Following are other situations or common bumps that athletes encounter on their journey, followed by some suggestions on what to do to help them get over the hill. These life lessons are necessary for helping players meet obstacles and challenges in the immediate future. Even more important, these teaching moments are crucial in ensuring that players learn to cope as they move beyond the playing field to adulthood. As the saying goes, "Nobody likes a quitter," and parents should understand that allowing a player to quit an activity, without great cause, is not admirable. Every effort should be made to work out a reasonable solution before even considering quitting, and all must realize there are times when players and parents have to make the best of an unpleasant situation. Many of these life-lesson situations follow with suggestions for parents and coaches on how to deal with them.

Physically Weak or Undersized Players

Over my twenty years of coaching, one of the most frequent concerns I would get from parents was that their son or daughter was small or had no strength. Unfortunately, some kids are not physically strong enough to succeed because of a lack of size or strength. This is a legitimate concern for parents because many of these physically weaker kids love playing the most. Often, they are among the hardest working and most fundamentally sound players. Encouraging small and physically weak players to continue playing and working toward their potential is suggested. Explain to them when they do grow and get stronger, they have a good chance of becoming one of the best players on the team. Usually around the age of fourteen, these players begin to grow and catch up in size to the other players.

There is no doubt that strength, speed, and power are important in sports. However, players should not take the fundamentals for granted. Many players' apparent lack of strength is actually a lack of good fundamentals. It may take a knowledgeable coach to notice, but without good fundamentals, strength rarely shows up. The fundamentals, when done correctly, give players the opportunity to put the most force into an object as often as possible. Players will grow and get stronger with strength training and conditioning, but increased power will not be evident if players' fundamentals are not solid. Good fundamentals are the best source of power and strength that any athlete can have. Fundamental development is an ongoing process and working with a good coach can be vital to developing perfect fundamentals. There are many undersized players at the highest levels of sports because they are fundamentally solid and have great determination. These players serve as a great inspiration for undersized young athletes, and parents and coaches can point these players out to the team members.

While players are working on fundamentals, there are strength-building exercises that will help players reach their full potential. Not every player can be a great athlete, but all can get stronger and negate the disadvantage of small size and weakness. Performing these exercises for an extended period will help with strength and with the mental discipline necessary to perform well. Remember, improvement at something comes with a daily routine focused toward a specific goal. Nowadays, many feel like the solution is weight training with a personal trainer. Although that is helpful and may be necessary at some point in a player's career, it is not necessary if players develop a simple routine to do at home or during practice.

Coaches can incorporate these strengthening exercises into the last ten minutes of each practice. In this age of growing concern over obesity, coaches should start incorporating a little conditioning work into practice time. Most people would be surprised by how much conditioning can be accomplished in just ten minutes. By starting this ten-minute program at a young age, it would become a normal practice routine as kids get older. Many young players will not do the exercises on their own but among their friends, and as part of their regular practice, they will. While doing the exercises, instruct players to imagine performing their playing skills with more strength and speed. The coach should not treat these exercises as punishment but as a part of practice—with the goal in mind of players getting stronger as the season progresses. It may be a good idea for the coaches to lead the exercises at first, and then let the players take turns being the leaders. Below is a sample routine that coaches can put into their regular practice.

Exercises for Players of All Ages to Add Speed and Strength

1. Much of the speed and control for athletes comes from the forearms, hands, wrists, and fingers. Players can work on these areas by squeezing things. There are many useful items on the market designed to help, but squeezing a tennis ball or water out of a towel will work just as well. Doing this a few minutes a day will develop the strength that will make a difference.

2. The next set of muscles to develop is the core muscles of the midsection. Doing fast hip turns while holding a weighted object are good. Gradual increases in weight held will develop this core strength. Old-fashioned sit-ups or any variation of those will be beneficial too.

3. Old-fashioned exercises like pushups are still great strengthening tools that are good for all ages. They will help develop the bigger muscles around the chest and shoulders. Performing different variations like hands wide, hands together, and fingertip push-ups will work on different muscles too.

4. Finally, doing lunges and knee bends will help develop the leg and rear end muscles, which are a major source of power. As players reach the junior high level, they can lift weights.

After a few weeks of this conditioning and continued work on the fundamentals, players will notice the difference. Finally, the best way to continue developing strength and power is to practice their skills more. Performing repetitions of the actual skills will lead to strength. For players who want to be their best, there is no substitute for practicing more than your competition.

The Unfair Coach

What can parents do? Remember, for parents who do not feel the coach is being fair, do not drag the player into it by stating your displeasure to the player. Often, the player is fine with the coach until the parent begins to make an issue of it. If the parents cannot get over their disappointment with the coach, a private talk with the coach may be necessary.

If a player cannot seem to get over the coaches perceived lack of fairness, a parent-coach talk may be needed too. Opening the conversation with a question like, "What can my son or daughter do to improve?" is effective and will not put the coach on the defensive. A casual talk with coach will usually solve things. Parents of high school age players should encourage the upset player to talk to their coach. This can be beneficial and a first step into adulthood for the player. Of course, parents should inform the player to be polite, but at the same time, they should state their concern to the coach and try to come to an understanding as adults.

Parents can explain to their kids that life is not always fair and encourage them to keep working hard. Explain that things will work out in the end if they work hard, whether the parent or player talks to the coach or not. Most of the time, parents and players are upset over a lack of playing time. This is a legitimate concern, but all concerned should realize that missing a little playing time, occasionally, is not going to affect the child's long-range future in the sport.

The Negative Coach or the Coach Who Ridicules Constantly

It would be great if coaches who coach in this manner did not exist or learned to be more positive, but unfortunately, there are some coaching our youth. What can parents do? First, parents have to gauge their child's reaction to the ridicule. All kids are different, with some handling criticism better than others do. When the child is not handling it well, a short talk with the coach may be necessary. If the parent perceives that the coach means well but has this negative way about him/her, then explain that to your child. The players may learn to live with the negativity and not take things personally. Parents might want to praise their kid's effort and hard work a little more than ordinary when they have this negative coach.

Coach Who Does Not Know the Game Very Well

What can parents do? Offer the coach your help. Extra practice with your own child or getting them outside-the-team instruction can be helpful so they do not fall behind for the future.

The Swearing Coach

Obviously, there is no place for inappropriate language in youth sports. What can parents do? A slip of the tongue here and there should be no big deal—tell your child that you do not condone it, but they will hear such talk the rest of their lives. Also, make it clear to them that it is language they should not use. The coach may use these words in his normal speech and may not realize he is using it with the team. A quick mention to the coach about his profane language, possibly in a funny way, may solve the problem. If this "salty" language continues and your child seems to be upset with it, the parent may have to inform league officials so they can deal with it. Some coaches at the high school level and above swear as a normal part of their coaching language. Although swearing is unnecessary, players of this age are usually adult enough to handle hearing it without any negative feelings. Many coaches who swear still have the best interest of their players in mind, so making an issue of it is probably not worth it at the higher levels of ball.

The Abusive or Borderline Abusive Coach (Physically or Verbally)

Unfortunately, some coaches go very close to the line or over the line of negativity into abuse. What can parents do? Parents should get a clear picture from their son or daughter of the situation and check with others who are involved (other parents and kids). Inform the league or school of your concerns and make sure they follow up on it. Looking into it immediately, before the situation escalates, is essential.

The "My Way or Highway" Coach

Some coaches have set rules and a set way of doing things with no bending of the rules or give and take on their methods. Sometimes these rules and methods do not seem reasonable for the players and/or parents and friction develops with the coach. This is another tough one to navigate for players and parents, because players do not want to get on the bad side of the coach. Many coaches who have this attitude have many years of coaching experience and are successful coaches. When that is the case and the coach seems to have the best interest of the kids in mind (at least in his mind), then everyone may have to adjust to the coach's philosophy. However, when the coach does not seem to have the best interest of the players in mind or is an inexperienced coach, then a talk with the coach may help let him know your thoughts.

When dealing with unbending coaches, explore other possibilities when possible. Other teams and coaches may be an option when a mutual understanding is missing between parents and coach. For high school players, there may be no other options if they want to play during the school year. I also do not believe a player should quit over this type of coach. As long as the player enjoys playing and this team will help their future in the game, it is worth living by the coach's rules.

The Uncaring, Swearing, Angry, or Problem-Creating Player

Some kids' hearts are not into competition and they usually stop playing at a young age. Most kids care, but they may not show it. Kids who have this "I don't care" or disruptive attitudes are either not successful, afraid they will not be successful, or feel neglected. Coaches and parents can try the following:

1. Give them some extra practice so they have a chance of greater success.
2. Try to get them to feel better about themselves with the suggestions in the "Building Optimism" chapter.
3. Give them extra attention, without neglecting other team members.
4. Talk to them one-on-one, showing you care and giving them options on how they can improve their attitude and help themselves and the team.

This type of player may even fall in love with the game when the player begins to have more attention and success. Any player, who is disruptive to the point where the coach has to spend an inordinate amount of time on them, must be brought to the parents' and league's attention. Ultimately, the parents (of the disruptive player) are responsible for their discipline.

Good Players' Attitude Toward Weaker Players

It is common for better players to get upset at weaker players' bad play. What can parents and coaches do? Coaches must recognize when a player (or players) becomes upset and shows their displeasure with their words or body language. It is a coach's responsibility to put a stop to players who "show up" any player over a mistake. Coaches should explain that it is the coach's job to talk to the player and they should leave the coaching for the coaches. For example, an often-used phrase in my coaching days was, "I'll do the coaching, and you do the playing." We also had a camp rule that prohibited negative comments. Only players, who never made an error or struck out before, which meant no one, could yell at someone else. Reminding players of this rule usually solved the problem, so players were quiet and did not show displeasure when others made mistakes.

In addition, I recommend that parents explain to their own child that not all players are good players, but all are part of the team and doing the best they can. Players should be encouraged to be understanding of their teammates and they should not display their displeasure on the playing fields.

"Me First" or "Know-It-All" Players

What can coaches do? This is part of a coach's to do list—trying to mold all different personalities and attitudes into the team concept. Some kids require more molding than others. Most players come around to the team concept with a persuasive and understanding coach. Teaching players that they are all an important part of the whole is an objective of the coach.

Players Who Have a Personal Coach

Many coaches do not like to hear that a kid will not do something because another coach told them to do it another way. This puts a young player in a difficult spot.

What can parents do? Parents should let their kid's team coach know their child is working with an outside coach, and the reasons why they are doing it. A good coach will not be upset or take it personally when a player is trying to better himself or herself. Coaches that are more insecure may get upset when players have another coach, so it may be best not to tell them about the player's personal coach. Parents should tell their kid to be open to all suggestions and to try what each coach suggests. Telling them to stay with what works best in the games is also advisable.

Coaching Your Own Child's Team

For parents who have the knowledge of the sport and can be fair with all team members, including their own, there is no reason not to coach your own kids. Parents who coach their own child's team need to separate the parent role from the coaching role during practices and games as much as possible.

☼ Other Things To Consider:

1. Be sure your child is fine with you coaching their team. The parent who is not going to coach may have to find out their child's real feelings about their spouse coaching the child's team. This may be necessary because the child may not want

to hurt their (coaching) parent's feelings, and therefore, do not state their true feelings to that parent.

2. Be sure to spend time with your son or daughter away from ball field and do not talk exclusively, or at all, about the sport when together.

3. Be sure to explain to your own kid your responsibilities as the coach. It may be necessary to explain certain game moves too, especially if your kid seems negatively affected by the moves.

4. For the parent who has coached their child for a few years, it may be good to step away for a year or so to let your child get instruction and a different situation from another coach.

5. Be open to, and seek feedback from, assistant coaches as to how they perceive things to be going between the coach and their kid. Coaches can be good counselors for each other.

6. It is important for the parent coach to remember they should not favor their own son or daughter with playing decisions, and conversely, they should not be tougher on their own child.

I, I, Me, Me

The following story is an example of a teaching moment that was seized upon by a player's family member. This true story is courtesy of one of the many fine coaches that I have had the pleasure of working with throughout the years. Coach Dan Fezzuoglio has told this valuable story to many young athletes, and it is a life lesson he had to learn in order to become the coach he is today.

> Like many athletes, who have reached the college level, Dan was one of the best players through high school. He had great success and often heard what a great ball player he was. Dan began to meet his match

in college ball. Although still a fine player, the competition had caught up to him. As happens to many athletes, Dan began to experience frustration with his play, and he let others know about the frustration by his excess actions on the playing field. When things did not go his way, he complained to the umpires, loafed when playing, argued with teammates, and moped when on the bench. His body language said it all and everybody at the games were well aware of Dan drawing attention to Dan. Little did Dan and everybody around him know that such antics were about to change.

Dan's older brother, whom Dan respected very much, came to watch him play one day. After observing Dan's egotistic behavior, his brother respectfully asked the coach if he could talk to his brother. The coach who was also obviously frustrated with such behavior said, "Sure." Behind, and up against the dugout, Dan's brother placed his index finger to Dan's chest as Dan's body slumped lower and lower. Dan's brother proceeded to say, "I am ashamed of watching you play that way. I cannot believe you would embarrass your team and school like that, and most of all, I cannot believe you would embarrass me and our family like that. If I ever see you act that way again on the field, I will kick the . . ."

From that day on Dan cleaned up his act and understood that he was not only representing himself, but also his family, team, and school. Dan admits that he was what he calls an "I, I, Me, Me," player up until that day. He admits that the talk changed his life for the better and is a lesson that he is adult enough to admit and pass on to others.

Heroes Come and Go, and Come Again

Years ago in professional baseball, I had a teammate who did not know how to read or write, at least not very well. For this reason, he, understandably, did not like to sign autographs. This player went on to have a very good major league career. Many years later, one of my students was talking about how an experience he had changed his attitude toward major league players and one player in particular. He said his feelings were crushed one day when he confronted his favorite player. One spring day, when the player was all alone on his way into the spring-training clubhouse, the young student asked his favorite player for his autograph. The player "blew him off" with some quick remark and disappeared into the clubhouse. I casually asked my student who the player was and he noticed my jaw drop when he told me. Yes, it happened to be the player whom I knew did not know how to write his name. After I told the student what I knew, he stood in amazement and left with a much better understanding. I am sure he never again spoke badly of his old baseball hero.

Things are not always what they appear to be or the way they are analyzed in the newspapers, on blogs, and on talk radio.

Going the Distance

You may recall in the introduction I said I wanted to share my experiences so I could help parents and coaches live up to the role model that you are. Well, it is true—you are a role model.

Recently, I attended a college orientation with my daughter. In the opening talk, I learned that when students were surveyed years ago, they listed their role models and heroes to be people such as John F. Kennedy, Martin Luther King, Jr., and famous athletes such as Muhammad Ali. However, students of today, by an overwhelming majority, list their moms and dads as their role models and heroes. My first thought was how cool that was. My second thought was not so cool; it was almost one of fear. I started to realize the great responsibility that being someone's role model carried with it.

Future Heroes

Finally, this book is for those whom I care most about and whom I have worked with the last twenty one years of my life— kids. I hope all young athletes have the great experiences they deserve to have as they grow up playing sports. These great experiences are only possible if parents and coaches live up to their role model responsibilities. Remember, "For it is what the teachers are themselves."

A Prayer with Life and Sport Perspective

Dear God: Help me be a good sport in this game of life. I don't ask for any easy place in the lineup. Put me anywhere you need me. I only ask that I can give you 100% of all I have. If all the hard drives seem to come my way, I thank you for the compliment. Help me remember that you never send a player more trouble than he can handle.

Help me, Oh Lord to accept the bad break as part of the game. And may I always play on the square, no matter what the others do. Help me study the Book so I'll know the rules.

Finally, God, if the natural turn of events goes against me and I'm benched for sickness or old age, please help me accept that as part of the game too. Keep me from whimpering or squealing that I was framed or that I got a raw deal. And when I finish the final inning, I ask for no laurels. All I want is to believe in my heart that I played as well as I could and that I didn't let you down.

    — A Poem by Cardinal Cushing, former Archbishop of Boston

Game Time

About the Author

FORMER MAJOR-LEAGUER, Jack Perconte, has worked with ballplayers for the past twenty-one years. His first book, *The Making of a Hitter,* is a critically acclaimed "how to hit" and "how to teach hitting" book. *Raising an Athlete* is Perconte's second book.

Illustrator, Bobby Delaney, is a graduate of the American Academy of Art.